WHEN GOODNESS FINDS YOU

LIVING A LIFE OF INTIMACY WITH GOD

Scott Boucher

WESTBOW®
PRESS
A DIVISION OF THOMAS NELSON
& ZONDERVAN

WestBow Press books may be ordered through booksellers or by contacting:

WestBow Press
A Division of Thomas Nelson & Zondervan
1663 Liberty Drive
Bloomington, IN 47403
www.westbowpress.com
1 (866) 928-1240

Because of the dynamic nature of the Internet, any web addresses or links contained in this book may have changed since publication and may no longer be valid. The views expressed in this work are solely those of the author and do not necessarily reflect the views of the publisher, and the publisher hereby disclaims any responsibility for them.

Any people depicted in stock imagery provided by Thinkstock are models, and such images are being used for illustrative purposes only. Certain stock imagery © Thinkstock.

All Scripture quotations, unless indicated, are taken from Holy Bible, NEW INTERNATIONAL VERSION®. Copyright © 1973, 1978, 1984 by Biblica, Inc. All rights reserved worldwide. Used by permission. NEW INTERNATIONAL VERSION® and NIV® are registered trademarks of Biblica, Inc. Use of either trademark for the offering of goods or services requires the prior written consent of Biblica US, Inc.

ISBN: 978-1-4908-5028-3 (sc)
ISBN: 978-1-4908-5027-6 (hc)
ISBN: 978-1-4908-5029-0 (e)

Library of Congress Control Number: 2014915688

Printed in the United States of America.

WestBow Press rev. date: 10/10/2014

CONTENTS

ACKNOWLEDGMENTS

Thank you, Lord. This book is only a reality because of your great goodness to me. It is for your eyes only! You are my witness—I wrote this book for you. Lord, you gave me the inspiration, wisdom, and creativity. You know, Lord, that I was willing to delete the entire manuscript so that only your eyes would ever behold this labor of love. Jesus—you are everything to me. I know that in your eyes this book is a masterpiece. That's all that matters to me—your eyes. May others be blessed because of your kindness to me.

I also wish to thank my family. First, my wonderful wife, Mary: Thanks for being respectful of me, and the enormous amount of time that I needed to finish this project. I promise you—this is not like the many projects and ideas I have had in the past—this is the real deal.

To my children, Josiah and Victoria: Thanks for understanding why your dad needed to be alone, night after night, to concentrate and pour his heart into this work. Each of you, in your own unique way, helped inspire me to write about the faith and innocence of a child.

Finally, a special thank you to my good friend John, who helped me edit the manuscript. You are a true friend indeed!

The Kingdom "Secrets"

*There are places in life we were never meant to venture into.
There is knowledge that exists, is widely sought after, and
yet was never designed to be known. -Boucher*

*"Call to me and I will answer you and tell you great and
unsearchable things you do not know." -Jeremiah 33:3*

$\mathcal{I}$am currently reading two great books on the "secrets" to
the abundant life Jesus talked about. The books are highly
inspirational and quite frankly, spiritually demanding, as they
should be. And now that I know the answers to the hard questions
concerning Kingdom life, I can share them with you.

Are you ready? The first and most important secret to living
victoriously in Christ is…. Follow…then…Wait a minute. I'm
not sure you are really ready for this. How do I know you won't
tell someone else this secret? How long have you been a Christian
anyway? I don't know if I can share such a deep truth with just
anybody. I better ask God if it's ok. If He says yes then I'll let you
in on our secret a little later in the book. But I'm not going to make
it obvious. You are going to have to work for it. I'll code the secrets
inside the sentence structure of a few hidden paragraphs. When
you think you have discovered the mystery phrase, turn to the back

of the book. No, the answer key is not provided. However, at the back is my address listing. Send a 3 x 5 self-addressed card to me and remember to write, "Please enter me into the 'Secrets of the Kingdom' mystery contest."

Then write down your newly discovered secret. In case of a tie, I will randomly draw one <u>lucky winner</u> (we don't actually use this phrase in Kingdom talk). I will pray and fast before a name is drawn. Of course all names are held confidential. All correct answers will be automatically entered into the grand prize drawing of a trip for four to the forbidden zone (the really deep side of the Kingdom). Actual prize may vary from that disclosed (after all, our God is a God of mystery). Actual cash value for lucky winner prize: $20 (or whatever you paid for this book). Cash value for grand prize: priceless. Hey, it took me over 25 years of searching as a believer to stumble across the keys to successful and abundant living, and I'm not giving them away for nothing.

Excuse my facetiousness for a moment. I hope you had a good laugh; I know I did while writing this. By now you should have asked the question, "what secrets?" Does God keep secrets from us that only some Christians ever figure out and get to enjoy? Would not the veracity of God come into question if He were to keep secrets from His own children? Is the Word of God only for the profoundly astute intellectuals in our ranks? Does the Holy Spirit lead us blindfolded by the hand in hope that we may someday stumble across the secret formula? Jesus meant it when he said, "But when he, the Spirit of truth, comes, he will guide you into **all** truth." (John 16:13)

You have probably read the books I mentioned that I'm reading now. There are hundreds like them that extol the Word of God, delivering its message with the outward appearance of a secret. These books are well written and help us in our walk with Christ. They have an alluring effect on us. We'll read or do anything if there is a chance we can drive away with the keys to a new life. When I first became a believer, I would have driven 24 hours non-stop just to hear someone preach a message about the keys to victorious living.

WOULD YOU LIKE FRIES WITH THAT?

We read fiction to dream; we read non-fiction to deal with reality. And when we read the latter, we look for the answers. That's why any book that offers the "secrets" is immensely popular. We chase after the keys to start the Victorious Living Car much like the world runs after mammon. Unfortunately, we often experience the same results. Our well-intentioned, laborious efforts last only to satisfy the present. Happiness replaces God's design for fulfillment. **God's wonderful, enthralling presence is all too often an experience rather than a living reality in our life.**

Our appetite for "secrets" has added fuel to the fact that the church has fallen for the lie that <u>one size fits all</u>. It's a theology that places a stamp on the new believer and sends him down the conveyor belt where he is packaged and gift-wrapped with a pretty bow. Then we rinse and repeat, rinse and repeat. This cookie-cutter mentality leads us directly into the express lane at the grocery store. It leads us through the drive-thru at the local greasy spoon. The sign reads, "Fast Food for the Hungry in Spirit". Don't go there! There is no fast food in God's Kingdom. Etiquette at our Father's banquet table, to a great extent, is a superior standard. A quick fix is deceitful, leaving the man of God devoid of all understanding of the fear of the Lord, the beginning of wisdom.

If the road to God's house doesn't pass by McDonald's, where does it lead? It leads us on a very lengthy treasure hunt. God exhorts His children when He says,

> My son, if you accept my words and store up my commands within you, turning your ear to wisdom and applying your heart to understanding, and if you call out for insight and cry aloud for understanding, and if you look for it as for silver and search for it as for hidden treasure, <u>then you will understand the fear of the Lord and find the knowledge of God.</u> (Proverbs 2:1-5)

In between the "if" and "then" you find out what is required of you if you are serious about pursuing God. You must accept, store up, turn your ear, apply your heart, call out, cry aloud, look for, and search for. Do all of this as if you were on a treasure hunt for precious silver, realizing you are sure to find the One who is more costly than gold.

This is hardly a quick fix or fast food meal. Agree? What's more, it's all available to us who believe. Jesus said, "Do not be afraid, little flock, for your Father has been pleased to give you the kingdom." (Luke 12:32) How much of it has He given to us? All of it! "All things are yours, whether Paul or Apollos or Cephas or the world or life or death or the present or the future—all are yours, and you are of Christ, and Christ is of God." (1Cor. 3:21) No secrets. None needed.

Having said all this, I'm not going to disappoint you. Every book needs to be clear in its presentation, resolute in the themes it offers to the reader. I will not speak of secrets. *Our quest to find the secret code in Christianity has led us down the wrong path. We have made it incredibly easy for someone to find God for the first time, yet extremely complicated to know Him much beyond that.* The keys are yours, nothing is hidden. Everything is free and accessible to you—Jesus' beautiful bride.

As you read this book, if by God's Holy Spirit he causes it to increase your hunger and thirst for the sweetness of His presence, I challenge you to take Him at His Word, press into God, and fill your cup to overflowing. **But buyer beware, you may tackle more than you could ever have dreamed of, and wake up one day to the wonderful intoxicating reality that is better known as Intimacy with God.**

CHAPTER 1

The Implied Word of Intimacy

Could it be that God's people are tired, worn travelers, who have come this far in the journey only to find that the road they have traveled is not too long or arduous—but something much more daunting? The confidence they once held in the joyful, innocent hearts of their childlike faith—has been replaced by an uncertainty wrought by a failed attempt to know, understand, and please God. Such weight truly is too great to bear.

*I*n my humble attempt to explain what an intimate relationship with God looks like, I must share with you something that sums up my feelings on this book you are reading. A. W. Tozer, pastor of Southside Alliance Church in Chicago for thirty-one years, wrote the well-read book, *The Pursuit of God*. In it, he said,

> **This book is a modest attempt to aid God's hungry children so to find Him. Nothing here is new except in the sense that it is a discovery which my own heart has made of spiritual realities most delightful and wonderful to me. Others before me have gone much farther into these holy mysteries than I have done, but if my fire is not large it is yet real, and there may be those who can light their candle at its flame.[1]**

---

[1]   A. W. Tozer, The Pursuit of God (Wheaton, IL: Tyndale House, 1982), 10.

I wrote this book for each and every one of you who dreams of knowing God intimately. I want to help you turn those dreams you have had for so long into reality, so you can experience God in ways you have never experienced Him before. This book is for those who long to experience and know God at a deeper level—who have always wondered how to make that happen. I wrote it for the ones who are tired of playing church—those who no longer wish to simply go through the motions and pretend everything is okay. If you have ever felt frustrated or disappointed by the fact that your relationship with God just isn't where it should be—this book is for you. And finally, for all those who can't identify with having these longings and desires—but truly want to experience God in simple, real, and heartfelt ways—here's your opportunity. If you are just simple enough to believe that God is good, then goodness will find you. If you are willing to come to Him in childlike faith, believing He is more wonderful than you could possibly imagine, then you will surely find intimacy with God.

I had searched many years as a Christian for a treasure map before I came to embrace the words of Solomon with contentment. "What has been will be again, what has been done will be done again; there is nothing new under the sun. Is there anything of which one can say, 'Look! This is something new'? It was here already, long ago; it was here before our time." (Ecclesiastes 1:9-10) Yet many years passed prior to my reluctant acceptance of this truth. I spent years of searching…and searching—more knowledge, more wisdom. I attended conferences to hear dynamic speakers. What I learned was good. It sustained me for awhile. But like Solomon said, "the eye never has enough of seeing, nor the ear its fill of hearing." (Eccl. 1:8b) Soon the ambiance wore off. "For with much wisdom comes much sorrow; **the more knowledge, the more grief.**" (Eccl. 1:18, emphasis mine)

Then I began to discover God on my own. I found Him when I was alone. I found Him when I searched with all of my heart. According to Tozer,

Sound Bible exposition is an imperative must in the Church of the Living God. Without it no church can be a New Testament church in any strict meaning of that term. But exposition may be carried on in such a way as to leave the hearers devoid of any true spiritual nourishment whatsoever. **For it is not mere words that nourish the soul, but God Himself, and unless and until the hearers find God in personal experience they are not the better for having heard the truth. The Bible is not an end in itself, but a means to bring men to an intimate and satisfying knowledge of God, that they may enter into Him, that they may delight in His presence, may taste and know the inner sweetness of the very God Himself in the core and center of their hearts.**[2]

I refer to this as the *great exhale*. When you experience what Tozer describes here, you will know exactly what I'm talking about. It's definitely worth a closer look, so let's take a peek at what intimacy looks like.

IDENTIFY WHAT YOU ARE LACKING

Do you ever feel like you wear a hundred different hats? Do your roles change weekly...daily...hourly? Take a look at your work environment or that of a typical supervisor. On Monday, you are the manager. On Tuesday, you have no choice but to play firefighter. You take the supervisor hat off because there are too many fires and no one to put them out. No time is left for your regular routine. On Wednesday, you are forced to be the babysitter. Someone is throwing a party, and he forgot to invite you. In order for the work to get done, against your wishes, you need to stand and watch your employees.

---

[2]   Ibid.

On Thursday, you become the counselor. Your time is spent giving advice—both professional and personal. On Friday, after racing to complete the projects, you might relax just a little in the afternoon and wear the hat of a friend. If you are fortunate enough to have the weekend off, you start the whole process over again on Monday morning.

Our relationships are often like the work situation I just described. We habitually fulfill a combination of roles, varying in degree by time and effort. Yet these are distinct roles that we have to play the part of—husband/wife, father/mother (sometimes both), son/daughter, brother/sister, uncle/aunt, grandpa/grandma, etc. Should I go on? I don't know about you, but I find the demands of life exhausting. We haven't even left the immediate family yet. When we move out a little from our immediate family circle, we fall into an array of relationships. We play the part of friend, neighbor, co-worker, and acquaintance. This, however, does not complete our circle of relationships. We change hats again through common activities and hobbies—adventures in work and play. This includes those we encounter through church ministry, Bible study, volunteer organizations, sports teams, educational advancement, and hobby clubs.

I'm a husband, father, friend, son, brother, uncle, neighbor, fellow Christian, Bible study leader, co-worker, and coach. That details the list of relationships that I am a part of. We're still talking relationships; we haven't even discussed the actual time spent at our jobs. In addition, there is the time spent working at home, church, and ministry. Where is the balance? How do we know how much time to spend in each of these areas of our lives? No wonder we are often overwhelmed and tired.

Do you have any time left? I doubt it. The next hat you will be asked to wear is the most important. That's the role you play as a child of God. The truth is that—there's no hat, and you can't play the part, though many do. When I get alone with God, my hats come off. I have no problem running to God and burying my head in His lap. Yet many of us just add our relationship with God to the list of life's duties and demands. You can't. It won't work. God will always be the one to get squeezed out. Don't make Him compete with the others on your list. He won't. He demands to be everything to you, and He's worthy to be. He supersedes life.

All of us struggle at some time in our lives with who we are and who we are to be. Often we just get busy living life, not really taking the time to consider our many roles or even address the struggle that exists. When we gave our lives to Jesus, it took each of us quite some time to discover who we were as children of God. When it comes to living out the roles that God has chosen for us, it's more than lost identity, low self-esteem, or lack of discovery that slows us down. There are plenty of self-help books and people crying, "Discover the voice of your inner child." Is it that simple? Do we just need to get in touch with who we really are? If that's true, I think some of us are in for a little disappointment. I don't know about you, but I'm not quite sure I want to get in touch with whatever is in there, let alone free it so it can get out.

All joking aside, there certainly are several voices talking. We can either listen to our own voices, the voices of the crowd, the voice of our enemy, or the voice of God. I'll stick with the latter. As I get closer and His voice becomes clearer, these roles in life become more meaningful, and my impact upon others becomes greater. The solution however, is not in the discovery of who we are, but rather in the discovery of who God is. That's where we need to start. The way to get there is simple to understand, yet difficult to do (because of us, not God). Much of the process has to do with the concept of approach, which I will discuss in length in chapter 4.

When we discover who God is, we will discover what we are lacking. It is then that we will also discover this thing of beauty called intimacy. This is the most important "role" to which you and I have been called as sons and daughters of God. *Often it is something implied, not stated. That's what makes it so difficult to talk about. It seems expected of us. The word is used in such a way that assumes the believer knows exactly what is being talked about, what it looks like, and how to get there.* Yet of all the roles we have, this one may be the hardest to explain. We kind of stumble as we think about what that would look like in our lives. Many would admit to not experiencing it. Others feel uncomfortable even talking about it.

Let's discover what we are lacking and find intimacy. First, we will define the subject of this book. *Intimacy is a close, on-going relationship where both partners are in full pursuit of the other. It involves a deep level of sharing as you bare your soul with someone you love. Feeling comfortable, you share your nakedness. There is an increasing level of trust. It is a song known only by you and your lover. This song is the expression of your love, written by the heart; penned both in times of intense grief and the unspeakable ecstasy of joy.* Jesus said, "To him who overcomes, I will give some of the hidden manna. I will also give him a white stone with a new name written on it, known only to him who receives it." (Revelation 2:17) That new name, known only to us, will serve as a reminder of the intimacy we shared with our Lord here on earth.

In his book, <u>Finding the Love of your Life</u>, Neil Clark Warren describes an intimate relationship that cuts to the core of one's soul. "The kind of intimacy I talk about involves the sharing of that which is innermost for two people, their deepest thoughts, feelings, dreams, fears and joys," says Warren.[3]

God, who is a relational being, designed us for the purpose of relationship. When we look at the relationship between a man and woman we see the similarities of God's design for intimacy with Himself played out in the romantic circle of an intimate marriage. If we study the main reasons why there is a lack of intimacy in most relationships between a man and woman, we can draw several parallels to the lack of intimacy that many believers experience with God.

---

[3]   Neil Clark Warren, Finding the Love of your Life (Wheaton, IL: Tyndale House, 1992), 104.

Warren cites three reasons for this lack of intimacy:

> **First, it's not a skill that most families teach their children during the developmental years. Life is so fast paced that there isn't much opportunity to sit down for long periods and communicate. Most individuals don't have time to figure out what's really going on inside themselves—let alone take time to share it with others…Second, our society is relatively blind to the importance of intimacy, so there is little reward or reinforcement for those who master this art form. People are paid more in our society if they produce well, given prestige if they get educated and deemed valuable if they look good…Third, intimacy requires a careful exploration of one's own inner world, and that's too frightening for some people. In our country there has been an epidemic of inattentiveness to the authentic, inner self, making intimacy virtually impossible.[4]**

How badly do you want God? Is He your heart's desire? Is He everything to you? Is He the one you dream and think about constantly? Is He greater than any other love in your life, so that everything else just pales in comparison? When someone looks at your life can they see that He's all you are living for?

Guess what? That's intimacy! When you begin to desire God in this way, you'll start spending more time with Him. You won't need to ask the question, "how much time?", because there really isn't any answer to it. I never give a definitive answer to the time question when I'm asked or when I teach a class on intimacy. You couldn't get enough of Jesus if you tried 24/7. Time is an important element, but really only a small portion of the solution. There are many religious men and women who spend hours every day in prayer, and don't

---

4   Ibid., 104-105.

really know God well at all. They would be better off reading a book or going to the beach. *Intimacy is not about time, it's about knowing someone. When you know someone intimately, you know what pleases them, and you know when they are pleased.*

So it is with God. He is not unreasonable, is He? When you know Him, you know the answer to that question. When God is pleased with you, you sense it in your spirit. You stop all that striving. You quit trying to please Him through endless works. Your soul lets out a giant exhale.

Some of us have been holding our breath for years, and we simply don't realize it. I love meeting people that are just learning to let out that first exhale. Such was the case several years ago, when I was teaching a course at church on Intimacy with God. After one of our final classes, I was approached by a delightful couple who had a question for me. This couple, in their mid-sixties, had been believers for 25 years, attending a bible believing church across town. With tears running down her cheeks, the woman said to me, "Do you teach any other classes here at church? My husband and I have never heard anything like this before. We want to take every class you are teaching." The freedom of intimacy brings relief to the soul. It has no choice, but to exhale.

Jesus said, "For whoever wants to save their life will lose it, but whoever loses their life for me will find it." (Matt. 16:25) And so it is for those who desire an intimate relationship with God. To the degree that you wish to save part of your life, to that degree you will not experience intimacy with Him.

One of the problems is that we don't live like Jesus means everything to us, like He is more important than life itself. We simply don't approach Him in that way. We think we can keep Him as a lifestyle, maintaining control of our lives. Then one day we will die, walk up to Jesus and say, "Thanks for saving me for all of eternity. I'm ready to serve you now. I'm ready to worship you. I'm ready to spend all of eternity thinking about you every second of my existence. I didn't choose to live life that way on earth, but I want to now."

Is that how it works? Is that Christianity? Are we to just live our own life, but love Jesus? Let's see…I have a good job…I have a nice house…my kids are healthy…my marriage is good. Oh yeah…and I love Jesus, of course. That's not Christianity. That's Americanism, with a little religion mixed in. If that is what you believe Christianity is, throw this book in the garbage can. You purchased the wrong one!

If your family is just as important to you as Jesus, you will not experience intimacy with God. Of course you may not admit it. None of us want to admit it. But take a look at your life. Could a casual observer of your everyday actions see that Jesus is clearly your all? Perhaps not, however, an intimate observer would get a clear picture. Could they tell that Jesus means everything to you? Or would they say that family is everything to you, but Jesus seems to be very important as well? Am I being a little extreme here? Let's look at what Jesus had to say about this.

In Luke 14 we read,

> Large crowds were traveling with Jesus, and turning to them he said: 'If anyone comes to me and does not hate his father and mother, his wife and children, his brothers and sisters—yes, even his own life—he cannot be my disciple. Suppose one of you wants to build a tower. Will he not first sit down and estimate the cost to see if he has enough money to complete it? For if he lays the foundation and is not able to finish it, everyone who sees it will ridicule him, saying, 'This fellow began to build and was not able to finish.' In the same way, any of you who does not give up everything he has cannot be my disciple. (Luke 14:25-30; 33)

What was Jesus saying here? He was saying,

> Hey, if you want to follow me, this isn't a one-time deal. It isn't going to be easy, and you need to decide beforehand that you are in this for the long haul.

> Wouldn't you consider the cost of building a tower, or house, or starting your own business? Then how much more should you consider the cost of making a life-long decision of following me!

That's actually the lighter part of what Jesus was trying to communicate to the large crowd that had been following him. Imagine the scene. The people had seen Him perform many miracles. Many had personally received God's provision. Fun wouldn't be enough of a word to describe what it was like to be a part of the crowd. It was exciting, mind-boggling, intriguing, and emotionally exhausting. The people were joyful, amazed, drawn, curious, and genuinely hopeful. There simply isn't the proper vocabulary to describe the experience. Their mind, will, and emotions, the very essence of one's soul, were overwhelmed by the very presence of the Living God. It was too much! His presence is all that we need, and yet it is more than any man can possibly handle.

Jesus knew by their wide-open eyes and passionate expressions that He had their full attention. So against the backdrop of this context, Jesus drops a bombshell on His followers. Let me put it in different words. He says,

> You are here because you see the miracles, so you've joined the crowd, perhaps looking for a provision for yourself. Whatever your reason, you have come to me. But now I ask you, 'Do you hate your parents, your children, and your spouse? Do you hate your life? Are you willing to give up everything you have? If not, then go home. You can't be my disciple!'

In Matthew 11:37-38, Jesus spells out the same thing to the crowd. He says, "Anyone who loves his father or mother more than me is not worthy of me; anyone who loves his son or daughter more than me is not worthy of me; and anyone who does not take his cross and follow me is not worthy of me."

Just imagine the look on the faces throughout the crowd. Most of them were still trying to comprehend what the Master had said the day before. Now he tells them that unless they hate their spouse and their own life, they can't be His disciple. Hate? What does that mean, they wondered?

I remember leading a Bible study several years ago when a member of our group mentioned the word "hate". Immediately a different member of our group spoke up. He said, "I don't like the word hate. I don't think we should even use the word. Do you know what that means? It means that you strongly dislike something. I think we should just say, 'I don't like that.'"

This man was attempting to not only change our vocabulary, but alter our way of thinking to serve the purpose of his own personal comfort. He was trying to take the sting out of the word, hoping that would lessen the wound caused by its piercing. Hatred is a hard thing to come to terms with.

That's why we look at these portions of scripture in a different way. We attempt to provide a cushion as a soft landing for the disciple so he won't get his feelings hurt or become offended at the words of Jesus, our master. Here's how we respond to it. We say,

> Boy, that Jesus sure has a way with words, doesn't He? I don't think He really meant it that way. You need balance in life. I think Jesus was saying that He should be #1 in our lives. That's all, nothing more than that. After all, my family is my life! My spouse and my children mean the world to me. They are a gift from God. There can't be anything wrong with that. They are the best thing that ever happened to me. Family is where it's at!

Listen, family is important to the non-believer as well. Non-Christians love their spouse and kids. That doesn't separate us from them. Christians should be different. Christ should be everything. **We don't lose our family by making this choice. On the contrary,**

we gain! Our spouse and children see that there is someone that we value far above them. And because of our devotion to Him, they feel secure in our love for them, and have a new level of trust and respect for God themselves. God doesn't ask us to make Him #1 in our lives—He commands us to make Him everything. Any man or woman who lives the kind of life that simply uses God for whatever pleasure they can get from Him, with the added benefit of salvation, has treated Him as a piece of merchandise.

David said, "Teach me your way, O Lord, and I will walk in your truth; *give me an undivided heart, that I may fear your name.*" (Psalm 86:11) There is a pathway to walking in the fear of the Lord. It is entered into by having an undivided heart. What is an undivided heart? Well, let's dream a little, shall we? First, think of your greatest joy, then your most precious possessions. Now think of your greatest desires, and the way you spend your time, money, and talents. Finally, what do you think about all day? This is what is important to you. To be undivided in heart is to set your affection on God, far above your affections toward everything else.

I hope by now you can identify what you are lacking. If you have a heart that is divided and you are setting your affections on everything else *but* God, it's time to make a change. Perhaps your experience of God has been frustrating. So what do you need? Do you need to change your experience of Him? Do you need to change your thinking? Maybe your theology is wrong? Perhaps your perspective is wrong, and you just need to start looking at things with new eyes?

There is hope for those who feel utterly hopeless. God is here right now to come through for you. Some of you are saying, "Really? Oh, please be true. I've been searching all my life. I know the Lord, but I'm weary and frustrated." Well, here's the moment you have been waiting for. Oh, storm-tossed child, the Lord speaks calm to your soul today. Freedom is not coming your way in the form of experience, thinking, theology, or perspective. You need the Lord; you need Jesus. **You need to know the security of His love.**

What do I mean when I say "know the security of His love"? You see, the Church has exhausted itself, laboring feverishly on one doctrine, that being the doctrine of salvation. Just look at the debate that has gone on for hundreds of years over the issue of eternal security. Yet there is something greater than knowing the security of one's salvation—it's knowing the security of God's love.

You will notice I didn't say that there is something greater in life than being saved. Every man and woman needs to be born again. But then we must move on as disciples to maturity. The question is not one of importance; it is one of purpose. The answer is found in the asking of this: What are we saved for? Some would answer that by describing our purpose in life once we receive God's free gift. They would speak of the Great Commission, or of love for our neighbor. Surely we are saved to serve and love others; that is correct. Yet there is a greater purpose. The Lord Himself answered the question as He prayed to His Father. "Now this is eternal life: *that they may know you*, the only true God, and Jesus Christ, whom you have sent." (John 17:3) Hence, we see the answer to our question: What are we saved for? We are saved for Him, to know Him. To love God with all our heart, mind, and soul, is to know Him intimately. When we know Him we become like Him. Do you want to be effective in your witness for Jesus? When others see Him, I mean really see Him in us, they will flock to Him in droves.

What man fails to secure through the frustrations of experience, is transmitted by a loving Creator in the form of an intimate knowledge of Him. It's on this firm branch that we build our nest. The blanket we have dragged along as a child has now been transformed into a beautiful gown that adorns our beauty in Christ. It becomes the framework for any future additions to the nest. We can lay our eggs in confidence. We pass on to future generations not the fact that we belong, but that we are loved.

Psalm 91:4 says, "He will cover you with his feathers, and under his wings you will find refuge; his faithfulness will be your shield and rampart." Why would you find refuge under His wings? That's because it's the place where your soul finds rest in His love for you. It's a place where you can watch the world go by. There is a place where you can exhale. It is a safe place to fail. It's the place where you can finally rest. This isn't heaven; it's right here—it's now. Put this book down and let out an exhale. Ask the Father to let you know how secure you are in His love. Lean your head into His chest and let your soul find its rest. If you live your life this way my friend—and you surely can—then you will no longer be bound by the worries and cares of this life.

It is the security of His love that proves failure meaningless. It renders it powerless. Sometimes you press hard, strive, and stumble, only to become even more disappointed in your walk with God. If you feel like your walk with God has been somewhat of a failure, there is something you need to know. Get to know the depths of God's love for you, and you will walk in success the rest of your days here on earth. It will absolutely transform you. And from the security of that intimacy, others will be blessed, and their lives changed. We comfort ourselves by reminding each other of the truth of our salvation, **but it is the security of His love, found only in the secret of our beauty to God, that brings joy, meaning, and hope to our lives.** This is the pathway to intimacy. You have just found what you were lacking!

CHAPTER 2

Garden of Longing

*It has been said that some men were created for greatness.
I say that great things were created for great men. God in
His foreknowledge created the man. He prepared a work
that only that man could do. God took great care in crafting
a work of beauty.*

*The work was too great for the man to conceive; too lofty for
his eyes to behold. So God took the man by the hand and
taught him His ways. He whispered into his mind and taught
man how to dream. All that remained was for man to step
into the greatness that was prepared for him. "For we are
God's workmanship, created in Christ Jesus to do good works,
which God prepared in advance for us to do." (Eph. 2:10)*

*Sometimes I feel like I just want to fall into a dream and
never wake up from that dream. I don't want to wake up
and have to face the harsh realities of this life, and the
disappointment of failed endeavors. Perhaps someday we
will all wake up to realize that this life that we now live
is but a dream.*

Do you like to dream? What's in a dream? Is it a longing in
your heart perhaps? How about a deep desire, a hope for
change, or an answered prayer? I'm talking to Christians here. You

still have dreams. Many of those involve becoming more like Jesus. At the end of the road in those dreams you will find and experience intimacy with God.

We have looked at identifying what we lack, and have defined intimacy. (Chapter 1) The realization of that lack of intimacy causes us to hunger and long for God's presence. That is where we will pick up our conversation here in Chapter 2. We will talk about how we long and dream for what could be, and what once was; that deep desire in each of us to return to a life of innocence. It is through this life of innocence and freedom that we will learn how to approach God in such a way that leads to an intimate relationship with the lover of our souls.

FINDING A WAY THROUGH THE DREAM

We are all just trying to find our way through life. Some of us might not even be aware of that, but it's true. Unfortunately for the majority of us, we rush expeditiously through this adventure called life. We don't take the time to smell the flowers, dance in the puddles, or linger at the crosswalk. We rush right past a thousand faces on our way to...nowhere. The beauty and delight of a dream is lost to the reality of a life of busyness.

I've watched my daughter several times from the front window of our house as she dances in the puddles during a rainstorm—with boots, a raincoat, and an umbrella. The funny thing is that she ran outside to do that a few years ago—when she was eleven years old! I think I'll join her next time. Oh—the simple pleasures that life provides! What an opportunity that has been bestowed upon us. If only we would allow ourselves the freedom to dance in the puddles, to linger at the crosswalks of life. But we are too mature for all of that, of course. That is how we think; that is who we are. Hence, the longings go unfulfilled; the dreams remain a wish that never comes true.

Indeed, we all have deep longings inside of us. Some of them are as simple as the desire to dance in the puddles. Most would admit that they are unsure as to what those longings really are. The reason we have a hard time identifying them is because we are largely unaware of who we are, and what we are to be. So we spend precious little time in pursuit of the discovery of these longings. The admission of their existence reminds us of the harsh realities of life—too painful, too complex, and extremely boring at times. We look the other way; we don't even want to consider it.

To find a way through the dream is to find God in the midst of the dream. Someone may say, "I have forgotten how to dream. I don't like to think about my days of innocence—they are gone. How can I return to a life of innocence and begin to dream again?" If that's you, I'm glad you asked. Here's the answer: *Find God in the midst of your dreams.* God can enable you to dream again. Set yourself free to allow the dreaming to begin in your life. First, you will have to believe you are free and innocent. Second, you need to think like one who is free and innocent thinks. Third, act like one who is free and innocent acts. Only the Lord can help you to do this. All of these things will, as you would expect, take time.

God calls us innocent because of what Christ has done for us. So God gives us the ability to live a life of innocence again. It is only possible in God, and it is only possible if we will believe. If you don't believe you can live a life of freedom and innocence, you will not think and act like one who is free. We must believe like a child and then take the steps of a child. The steps of a child are faith, trust, freedom, joy, and innocence. We will discuss this further in chapter six when we discover the five keys to intimacy with God.

Consider the life of Joseph we read about in the book of Genesis. Joseph was sold into slavery at a young age by his own brothers. He ended up in prison after being wrongly accused by his master's wife. He lived for years in a dungeon! (Gen. 40:15) How could Joseph ever return to a life of innocence after many years of hardship, the loss of family, and the marked deprivation of his childhood years? We find the answer in Genesis 41:51. Joseph named his firstborn Manasseh and said, "It is because God has made me forget all my trouble and all my father's household." God made Joseph forget. Instead of entertaining bitterness, he embraced love and forgiveness. Instead of living in despair, Joseph chose to anchor his soul to hope. And God responded by enabling Joseph to forget about all his troubles; to live a life of innocence as if none of it had ever happened. Because *when goodness finds you,* God causes you to forget all the troubles you once had, and fix your eyes on the overwhelming kindness He has now poured out on your life. Joseph never gave up on his dream.

One dream—just a simple dream. Are you not glad that your heavenly Father likes to dream? I'm glad He didn't stop there. He spoke the dream into reality, and presto—you and I appeared onto the scene. We became a part of His story. Now we must find our way through this dream that has become a reality. To experience intimacy with God, you must learn how to dream again. *To dream is to allow your heart to be filled with hope.* Once you begin to dream again, you will get in touch with those deep longings you have, and you will have a desire to return to your days of innocence.

Mankind suffered a loss of innocence, beauty, and knowledge in the Garden of Eden. Unfortunately, we often take the longing we have for Garden of Eden-type living, replace it with emotional experiences, and begin a long quest for greater beauty and knowledge. It all culminates in a futile attempt by mankind to gain a sense of control, a stronger footing on the path where we once had a strong foundation. Innocence, freedom, and joy, however, are not gained through beauty and knowledge. But they can be found as you take the steps of a child and walk in intimacy with God.

INNOCENCE LOST

Let's look at how innocence is lost, and then we will search out ways to return to it. It's painful to think of how innocence is lost.

The pain is real and the scars are deep. The wounds occur through various circumstances. By the time we reach middle-age, innocence is a distant memory, largely because we choose to allow it to become such. It's not a matter of being innocent one day, and the next we are not. Don't think in those terms, it will just confuse you. Neither is it right to think in terms of age. Innocence is not merely a vague state of mind. There are unmistakable, tangible periods throughout our lives, including adulthood, where innocence can be lost.

In general, the loss occurs in these ways: betrayal of trust, introduction of evil, pain of rejection, and removal of the familiar. There are unquestionably more, and some of these overlap, with many sources. Briefly, I describe the cause behind each category of loss below. This is by no means a complete list. The brevity here does not do the subject justice. But it gives us a foundation to work with.

Betrayal of trust—trust that was established in early childhood, or trust that was developed in relationships. Source—abuse, lies told by the parents, gossip, and abandonment. This may include trust that is betrayed in a marriage relationship, whether or not it results in a divorce.

Introduction of evil—the physical point, event, or day when the line was crossed; the open door through which access was allowed. Source—various: knowledge, education, abuse, and false doctrinal belief. It often comes in the form of what we put before our eyes, and in our ears. It begins in childhood, and continues into adulthood. Evil enters by way of media, music, art, literature, and the influence of specific individuals.

Pain of rejection—events that triggered loss, or bring harmful memories due to loss incurred. Source—dating or marital relationships, playground rejection by peers, lack of love or attention from parents, and loss of job or inability to find employment.

<u>Removal of the familiar</u>—everything you know is taken away from you; the young bird is forced out of its nest of protection. Source—a sudden and painful change in one's environment; you lose your sense of security due to uncontrollable circumstances. Children: loss of parents, abandonment, and change of school due to family relocation. Adults: loss of employment, sudden catastrophic loss of belongings, loss of health, and divorce.

Imagine it as a sink full of water, where water represents innocence. Did you ever reach your arm into the water, slightly pull on the drain plug, and just let a little flow out? The seal is tight, the pressure is great. Now the level is less. If the drain plug is not perfectly in place, the water continues to seep out. You go into the next room and get preoccupied with doing something else. When you return, you notice the water is all gone. How could that have happened? It was so quick, so subtle, and such a setback.

Well, in this case you just fill the sink with water again. Secure the drain; start the dishes. It's no big deal. You forgot about it already. It's not that way with innocence. In fact, most people just stare into the empty sink of their lives and think it will never be the same. They cannot imagine a life so full and free. How can a heart that has been hardened by life's cruelties, become once again a thing of joy and beauty?

INNOCENCE RECLAIMED

How do we regain this lost innocence? Answer: We become like a child. This return to innocence begins on the day we give our lives to Christ and become born again. But it doesn't stop there! We can live a life of innocence by walking in the freedom God has given us. In chapter six, we will discuss the restoration of innocence much further, with practical ideas on how to live this way in your own life. But since we are talking about longings, let's prime the pump a little here and give you a taste of what lies ahead.

We start by observing little children, in the hope that we can emulate the kind of behavior that would draw us closer to God. It's interesting as we observe children, that we notice so many of our Creator's characteristics in them. God, our Father, has truly created us in His image. We can make these general observations about children: they quickly forget an offense; they are innocent in their knowledge of evil; there is a complete trust in their parents' ability to protect and provide for them. The eyes of a child are filled with wonder. Children believe what they are told without a thought of doubt. There are no worries, cares, or burdens they bear. They are free from all fear of any kind.

Little children dance and delight in the simplicity of life's wonders. They have an unshakable faith in their parents. Their hearts are free from inhibition and animosity, which keeps them tender and open. And here's one that is going to make a vast impact on our future relationship with God—children boldly approach their parents with an expectation of something good. Is it no wonder that God's desire for each one of us is to have the faith of a little child?

Do you want to walk in this kind of innocence and faith before the Lord? How do you reclaim it? You simply do the things I just mentioned. Begin to develop the faith of a little child. Maintain a heart that is tender and open. Ask God to help you to dance and delight in the simplicity of life's wonders. It may seem like a daunting task. But with God's help it is possible, one small step at a time.

CHAPTER 3

Misplaced Theology

We were made for His presence. But something has happened. Sin has not only robbed us of fellowship with our Lover, it has engendered a society of second-handed people pleasers. A remnant indeed, yet a people that are more familiar and content to offer sacrifice, than to face the awkwardness of approach that intimacy with God requires.

*L*et's take a look at the misguided theology that has become a substitute for intimacy. We will do that in three parts: A) The ABC's of Christian Growth. B) A Lack of Understanding. C) False Assumptions. In some instances, it is not necessarily a substitute, but rather a severe limitation on our ability to experience that desired intimacy.

THE ABC'S OF CHRISTIAN GROWTH

What did I mean by the statement that I made earlier about the Church falling for the lie that teaches "one size fits all"? It's very simple. We teach new believers the golden rule that we have been taught ourselves: prayer, studying the Word, and fellowship. Those are as basic as the three 'R's (reading, writing, and arithmetic), are to schoolchildren. However, one size does not fit all. These are the main disciplines for a Christ follower—absolutely—yet each of us experiences God in a different way. This is often overlooked, therefore delaying growth that should occur early in the development of a disciple. Each of us tends to look through a slightly different lens; we become a Christian and now we must learn to see ourselves through the lens of God's camera. We know that 1 + 1 = 2. Jesus + me, however, that just doesn't seem to mix well. Concern enters our hearts when we attempt to solve the equation. One understands the ingredients, but the end-product is hard to envision. We can't visualize a sum on the other side of equals. We fail to see the wholeness of a life so broken as our life is. We thoroughly understand the basics, so now what? What's next for the believer?

How do we describe to a new disciple what the life of a sold-out follower of Jesus looks like? What should it look like? Few know, because there are hardly any mentors. In our theology we embrace salvation, and rightly so. We approach the equation and teach what we know. It's good, yet it never seems to go far enough to give the believer victory in his life. It never seems to do enough to remove the burden, to destroy the yoke. (Isaiah 10:27) *What we don't teach is something that can't be taught: a) How to approach God. b) How to know God. c) How to desire God. d) How to hear His voice. e) How to dance with God. Yet it can be mentored to others. And when they see it in you, they will know it is what they have been searching for their entire walk with the Lord.*

My friend Jack is the intellectual type. He loves to talk about deep spiritual and philosophical issues. I have enjoyed many conversations with him throughout our years of ministry and friendship together. I simply enjoy just hanging out with Jack, as he is fun to be around. He had already been a believer for many years when I asked him if he was experiencing intimacy with God. He replied, "I'm not intimate with God right now. I haven't been in the past, and I'm not really even sure what that is. I don't know how to get that."

Here stood my good friend who could debate any topic in Christianity with much enthusiasm and ardor. Jack, a man suitably trained in scripture, was at a total loss for words. As I searched a little deeper, I found out that he never was able to gain a proper view of God as his loving Heavenly <u>Father</u>. He just couldn't relate to Him as such. This compounded the fact that he was never mentored in his walk with God. Jack understood and embraced the foundational teachings on salvation. He was at every worship service, Bible study, and fellowship gathering. But somewhere along the way, he struggled in his approach with God. Somewhere along the path, he missed out on intimacy. So I could not talk to him in terms of *desiring God, hearing God's voice, or dancing with God.* These were all foreign concepts to him.

I'd like to say that after we prayed Jack went on to have a meaningful, intimate relationship with God, but I can't. I'd like to say that Jack is the exception in Christianity, but I won't. I'd like to say that most believers are experiencing a deep intimacy with the Lord today. If it were true, I wouldn't have written this book. The truth is that I find a lack of intimacy to be the common thread.

So what do we do? *We find out where people are at in their growth and development, and start from there. The ABC's never change—they get better, stronger, and deeper. Our prayer life gets more intimate. We dig our roots deeper into God's Word. We begin to love others deeply, from a genuine, pure and unselfish heart.*

Once we know where people are at, we start to teach them, to help them move to a deeper walk with God. We build an atmosphere where desire can be cultivated in an individual. When we sense desire building we immediately, with great care, feed that desire. Then we look for mentors for those with such a desire. What we never do is assume that "one size fits all". We also don't pretend that growth will take place automatically.

THE NEED FOR MENTORS

When true intimacy is properly modeled, all those who live their life in some form of surrogate intimacy will be drawn like a magnet to the real deal. The church has never had a greater need for mentors. Not merely good role models, but preferably men and women that genuinely care for your soul. They are hard to come by. Most believers are too busy to get involved in the trench work known as discipleship. Yet nothing is effective in discipleship compared to the process of mentoring. Many have had mentors in other areas of life (i.e. education, parenting, business), but not in the area where it matters the most.

How were you raised? I don't mean by your parents. How were you raised in the Lord? Who discipled you? Were you discipled at all? Was someone there at your side, modeling the very life Christ wants us to lead? Or were you left on your own, forced to play the Christian survival game? When I was fourteen I was led to Christ by a family friend. He left me with a tract to read. I don't remember ever seeing him again.

The Church of Jesus Christ seems to have drawn a line in the sand concerning the gospel of salvation. Normally a line in the sand would represent a good thing—an unwillingness to compromise on our beliefs. However, in this case it represents a finish line, a sudden climax to the race.

We have made it our goal to get sinners saved. The result: great for the Kingdom's initial and most important phase—salvation. Where we seem to drop the ball is in a placement of emphasis on the second and third phase of our new life in Christ. Much like natural birth, phase two is the immediate care of the newborn child.

We've packaged it so well that there's almost no need for parents anymore. All you need is a do-it-yourself kit. Here's a tract containing the four spiritual laws. Read it, pray the enclosed prayer, and hopefully send us your address so we can send you some further literature.

It's easy, perhaps too easy. Not only do we neglect to properly care for the newborn believer, we assume they will enter phase three (the growth and maturity phase) on their own. When it doesn't happen, we respond shockingly to the news that our new brother is stunted, struggling to grow, or sadly—just not growing at all.

What went wrong? We, the Church, are like a football team stuck at our own ten-yard line. We could score if we could just manage to get out of the huddle. The problem is that we think the goal line represents salvation, so we place all of our emphasis, effort, thinking, teaching, and preaching on the attainment of that goal. Salvation is already represented in team membership. You wouldn't have the team uniform on if you hadn't received the gift of Christ. In this case, not belonging to the team will cost you more than the loss of this game of life. It will cost you your eternal soul. But the goal line isn't salvation—it's having an intimacy with God; it's about knowing Christ so intimately that you become a mature, fully devoted follower of Jesus. A lack of understanding about these concepts has encouraged people to fall for this lifestyle of surrogate intimacy.

As the bible teaches, we need to move on past the elementary teachings, of which salvation is listed as belonging to:

> Therefore let us leave the elementary teachings about Christ and go on to maturity, not laying again the foundation of repentance from acts that lead to death, and of faith in God, instructions about baptisms, the laying on of hands, the resurrection of the dead, and eternal judgment. And God permitting, we will do so. (Heb. 6:1-3)

The goal is maturity, that's why we need mentors. They do their work, "until we all reach unity in the faith and in the knowledge of the Son of God and become mature, attaining to the whole measure of the fullness of Christ." (Eph. 4:13)

My wife and I are blessed with two wonderful children. Though they may question from time to time the depth of our love for them, they know with a certainty that they belong to us. In fact, it is out of this freedom that they can explore the depths and validity of their parents' love. This is the point at which we, God's children, tend to get stuck. There is a sense of reluctance on our part to move on from the doctrine of salvation and approach or tackle other aspects of this wonderful relationship with God, such as developing intimacy with Him. There is no lack of desire to do this. We would love to pull hard on the doorknob, swing open the closet door, and open our eyes to a vast abundance of treasure revealed in intimate knowledge by the Lover of our souls.

We're just afraid to open the closet door. It's dark in there. We hesitate as we cling to our blanket we have been dragging around the house for years. We cling to the blanket of salvation because we feel so comfortable with it. It's what we know best. And we know no one is going to disapprove or take it away from us. After all, salvation is the most important thing. So we have to start there; we always need to preach salvation as the starting point. But it's time to grow up.

We do this not by leaving childhood behind. Rather, from the secure standpoint of knowing one's salvation and being confident in whom we belong to, we embrace the freedom of exploring the depths of the Father's great love for us through an intimate, romantic relationship with Him. This journey leads us not to the state of adolescence or adulthood, nor to the high plateau of experience. The journey leads to a place of rest, a place of peace, contentment, and joy; a place where the child of God is settled, not fidgety or full of striving.

It is no wonder that I meet Christians who have been following the Lord for fifteen or twenty years and yet have no clue as to what intimacy with God is. Many believers do not know how to obtain it, hence the reason why I chose to write this book. Several years ago I ran into a woman I had known for quite some time. She used to attend the same church where I was a member. In the course of our conversation, I mentioned my desire to write a book about intimacy with God. Her jaw literally dropped wide open as I spoke the words. She said, "Do you have the heart of David?"

How is one to answer that question? "Uh, yeah—of course I do!" Or would it be more humble to say, "No, not me." I knew what she meant by her question, but I was very concerned about something she didn't say. Behind her question was this deceitful, wayward thought: "Intimacy is only for some; you need to have a heart like David's. Only special, chosen believers have that kind of heart. I've been a believer for many years and I don't have that intimacy, so I probably never will."

Are her thoughts yours? Do you find yourself longing for intimacy, but not really believing you will ever taste of it? Perhaps to you it is a distant memory, or a one-time experience. For every one or two that break through to intimacy, there are a hundred that never do. Many just stop short and live in this land of substitutes, this place of surrogate intimacy. With more mentors, we will see an increase in those who experience breakthrough.

If you have never been mentored, it's not too late! The ideal situation would be to find a mentor from the very start, shortly after you give your life to Jesus. Your need to grow as a disciple, however, never ceases or diminishes. What does that mean? It means you need someone there at your side speaking into your life just as much today as you did when you first gave your life to Christ. You may be fifty or sixty years old, and have walked with Jesus for thirty years, but that doesn't matter. The mentor's instructions to you will be at a higher level, but the need never changes. We desperately need each other in the body of Christ. We all need someone to encourage, strengthen, instruct, and challenge us. This is the wind that keeps our sails full.

Pray for the Lord to send a mentor your way; pray also for God to make you a mentor to someone else, and be looking for that opportunity to help disciple your brother or sister in Christ. Your love and support will be exactly what they need to break free from the prison and downward spiral that are a consequence of surrogate intimacy.

A Lack of Understanding

You are what you eat. This is a popular saying that few would attempt to refute. We know conclusively what happens to our bodies when we lack self-control, and make poor eating choices. My wife will tell you this is still an area I have not mastered. In fact, as I write this I just ate a whole can of Pringles in about ten minutes. I doubt if that's going to help me health-wise. But it sure tasted good; it's hard to just eat one or two chips. We all know the effect that certain foods will have on our bodies because of the abundance of knowledge we have in the area of health today. Add personal experience to this, and it enables each of us to be an expert of sorts.

How then is it that we fail to see the warning signs of an unhealthy spiritual diet? To answer that, let's go back to my first statement. *You are what you eat.* Add this—**you become what you know.** Do you want to become an "expert of sorts" in your knowledge of God? Do you desire to have a thriving relationship with Jesus that resembles what He called the "abundant life" in the scriptures? Then you need to begin by asking yourself, "What do I know?" I'm not talking about mere head knowledge here.

How does a lack of understanding place a limitation on your ability to experience intimacy? The best way I can put it is that you become intimate with things or people in your life, not God. You have become what you know. You have an intimate knowledge of the people and things in your life. But your lack of knowledge about God keeps you at a distance from Him. *You limit your own ability to know God because you simply have a finite amount of time, energy, and desire in life and it is being spent elsewhere.* Then you come to a situation in life where you need to make a decision or have help to make it through a difficult time, and you are found lacking. You don't sense His presence or peace; you lack the knowledge and understanding of His ways. You're confused; you don't know what decision to make. In this state you lack the intimacy with God to approach Him in faith and confidence, receiving from Him what you need to get the victory in the storm you are facing. In the book of Hosea, the Lord said, "my people are destroyed from lack of knowledge." (Hosea 4:6) Have you ever been so confused, you didn't know what to think? When you are in such a state, this lack of understanding becomes a cloud that limits you from walking in intimacy. With a clear understanding of who God is, what His good plans for you are, and what He wants to accomplish in your life, you can march right through the thickest fog.

Several years ago I was with a friend who was faced with making some major decisions. The decisions he was about to make would alter the course of his life. He had painstakingly thought about the reality of the options that lay before him. The finality of it all shook him. Deep in thought, he turned to me and said, "Scott, I just don't know what is true anymore."

There is a place where truth, and that which we thought was truth, meet. It is a place of confrontation. Like my friend, we get to a place in our lives where nothing makes sense to us. The control that we hold onto so deeply gets shattered. It's more than a mere reality check. The truth that we call "our life" collides with a greater truth. Many of us identify this experience as simply reality, nothing more. But for the believer, they know it is the truth of God's Word that stares them in the face. Well, then the decision becomes obvious. It becomes a matter of obedience. That means giving up control of our life to God. This includes our time, thoughts, desires, and every way we live out our daily life. It requires a commitment to raising our level of "knowing God", a commitment to growing in our understanding of His purposes.

Let's back up a little. Before you allow the experiences in your life to resemble a car wreck, there's something to take a deeper look at. As I stated, *you become what you know.* Did you ask yourself the question, "What do I know?" We are all experts at something in life. Think about it. You spend 24 hours a day doing a number of things. You have been performing those tasks for years. A wealth of knowledge has come with that experience, literally thousands of hours. Your expertise may lie in your field of employment, parenting, marriage, cooking, sports, or many other areas. When you spend so many hours studying a subject, you know it well. What do you think about all day? Some would answer—nothing. Unless you're a zombie, I disagree wholeheartedly. The subject you study could be your spouse, your physical beauty, children, hobbies, or television.

Your diet becomes who you are. In this case it's not physical food, but it's a steady diet of thoughts, desires, and knowledge. I know a few people who talk about the weather every time I see them. I would like to ask them, "Is that all you think about? Why do you mention the weather to me every time our paths cross?" I used to be so self-absorbed with sports—it was idolatrous. I could drive my car for an hour or two and remain in deep thought about my favorite team, as if I was their coach. I would think about players, strategy, upcoming games, and transactions that could make the team more successful. I knew the statistics of the top players by heart. I had become what I knew. It was what came out of my mouth, because it was on my heart and in my mind constantly. I was a Proverbs 23:7 man. "For as he thinketh in his heart, so is he." (Proverbs 23:7a KJV)

This may not be something you consider as competition with God. The time, money, and desire you pour into these areas of your life, however, will eventually become your treasure. And we know how Jesus cautioned us against this. "For where your treasure is, there your heart will be also." (Matt. 6:21)

So where does the lack of understanding come in? Simple—follow the path with me. You become what you know; you are what you eat. If your heart, mind, emotions, and time are focused on the affairs of this world, that's who you are. It's what you think and talk about, and what others say you are. You have become what you spend all of your time getting to know, in an intimate way. This results in a lack of understanding about what your soul really desires—an intimacy with God. You have substituted something else in its place. It could be good things—relationships, family, etc. There are only a limited amount of things you can really know well (because of time requirements). By your own choice, you have applied your time to some endeavor in this life. Now you are left with an inadequate amount of time to develop an intimacy with God. So you end up lacking an understanding of God and His ways—you know little of God. *Many Christians spend the majority of their time in this life getting to know things they were never meant to know.*

If you are seeking God's Kingdom first, then your mind is on His things daily. No matter how busy you are, or what task you are doing, you spend your time dwelling on Him. If you do this even in the midst of playing with the kids, doing dishes, or driving the car, you will certainly grow in your knowledge, and more important— your experience of God. You will become what you know; you will grow in intimacy with God. It doesn't need to be 24/7. Who do you look to in your job, relationships, and family? Your thoughts should reveal that God means everything to you. If He is 2nd, or 3rd, or 5th— something is wrong. If your job, family, sports, television, or hobbies are more important, then something has to change. Praising Him, praying, and meditating on His Word can become like brushing your teeth; it can become routine. This is where we need to get to in our walk with God. If you are not there, don't freak out, condemn yourself, or panic.

The life I am talking about is in stark contrast to the life story of many Christians who don't talk much about the Lord. They talk about everything else. It's the things they have been putting inside of them that are coming out. If this is you—there's hope! You can change today. You don't need to beat yourself up with contempt and guilt. You don't have to wait for God to be willing to take you in. That's the story of God's love and goodness.

Start right now. First, confess who you are. This is what you have become, because of what you have decided to gain an intimate knowledge of. Second, repent of your lack of knowing God. Repent of your desire to know everything instead of Him. This includes spending countless hours on things that simply have no eternal purpose or value. Third, don't stand outside the gates of heaven like some unworthy servant. You are His son; you are His daughter. Run past those gates right into the throne room, straight into the arms of your loving Father. Fourth, resolve to know Him now, above everything else in your life. Formulate a plan so you can carry out this resolution. For instance, how are you going to spend your hours, days, and weeks? How are you going to renew your mind? (Then what you know will change.) This may require a change in atmosphere and/or relationships to accomplish.

Finally, the fifth step is confessing who God is. Start with God is good, and run down the long list of His wonderful attributes. Meditate on them daily. No longer will a lack of understanding keep you from intimacy. And when you find yourself again standing outside the gates, in discouragement, depression, and fear—make a choice. Run into the inner courts and jump into His arms like any confident child would do. You are worthy because of Jesus to be there. You are a co-heir with Christ; you belong in God's family. Start acting like it. Believe it, live it, and enjoy it.

FALSE ASSUMPTIONS

There is a common expectation put on new believers. As I have already mentioned, it is taken for granted that if they follow the formula of prayer, fellowship, and studying the Word of God, things will fall into place, and growth will occur. The expectation also includes a belief that people will just know how to relate to God, as if it will be automatic and natural.

Let's admit it, how often have we said the following to someone who just came to Christ? "It's easy, just don't forget—prayer, God's Word, and fellowship—and you should be alright." Then with a slap on the back, our new convert is merrily sent on his way. It should be of no surprise to us, three years later, when we find the new believer drinking milk instead of eating meat. Today the "easy believe-ism" of the gospel presentation is followed up with a crash course introduction to God.

I believe we have made a serious mistake in adhering to this philosophy. **We have set people up to fail; we have laid a trap of frustration and disappointment for the disciple.** We do right by pointing new believers to the simple path of maturity. As I stated previously, the basics of prayer, Bible study, and fellowship never change. But then we cover the path with a thin layer of false assumptions. Later on we find ourselves surprised by the fact these disciples are not as far down the path as we think they should be.

Growth will surely occur as we, the disciple, remain plugged into the vine (Christ), and are led by the wisdom and guidance of the Counselor (Holy Spirit). However, our God "is a consuming fire" (Deut. 4:24). No one gives matches to a child and expects him to build a bonfire. Instead, we tenderly care for and nurture the child, and God causes the growth. Experience changes the boy into a man, and there is much wisdom and confidence gained along the way. There are things to learn and things to observe. Nothing should be taken for granted. In the same way we learn to rightly handle fire, we must learn how to approach and relate to this God who is a *consuming fire*.

There are too many assumptions that we make in the body of Christ. A mixture of false assumptions between the pulpit and the pew can result in a serious disconnect. Many years ago I was involved in leadership in a church I used to attend as a young adult. After a sermon one Sunday morning, I had an eye-opening conversation with a friend who also attended that same church. He confessed, "I feel like every time our pastor speaks he assumes that the rest of us are living in sin. It seems his messages are developed with this in mind. I feel he is pointing his finger at us."

Wanting to defend the pastor whom I loved, yet willing to patiently listen, I remained quiet. "Shame on you—you need to repent. That's what I get from his sermons," he added. I wanted to ask my friend if indeed he did need to repent. But I resisted the desire to do so. Even if his claims were true, and I doubt they were, I was not the person with whom he should be discussing it. He needed to go directly to the source.

Perhaps we have erred by separating the altar from the pew. I'm sure there are a few assumptions that are made both ways. However, none are more obvious or dangerous than the false assumption that many believers make that goes something like this: "My growth in Christ is the responsibility of my pastor and the leaders of my church. It is their job to bring me a word from God and tell me how God is leading me and what His will is for my life." Although few would admit to thinking these thoughts, and far less would dare to speak them, they are often borne out by their actions.

One of the biggest assumptions that many Christians make on a regular basis, often unwittingly, is the assumption that they will grow if they just show up for church every Sunday and spend ten minutes a day reading the Bible. The more precarious assumption that occurs is the belief that this is ok. It's not ok. It is a lazy approach to walking with God. Often the believer just falls into the habit of living this way. They assume this sort of lifestyle is not really a big deal with God. It is a big deal, especially for someone who has been walking with God for any significant length of time. God expects more from a believer who has been fed, nurtured, and ministered to for years.

Lastly, we assume that as long as we are saved, the rest doesn't really matter. It does matter. Why? It matters because we were created to give God glory. Our very existence is for the express purpose to give God glory. And when we live like it doesn't matter, we rob God of the glory He could have received. False assumptions are deceptive. They lead one to live a life that bears no fruit for God's glory.

CHAPTER 4

Learning How to Approach God (Getting Comfortable in His Presence)

*The altar of worship is regularly **approached** by God's elect, but seldom laid upon. Thus it becomes a lovely place to visit, but a lonely place to stay. Every man walks in the loneliness of his soul at some point in his life. Yet the man acquainted with loneliness does not have to walk in depression and discouragement. The man who has never walked that lonesome path must ask himself what path he has ventured upon. For the cause of Christ not only pierces the soul of man, it shatters every fiber of understanding a man can cling to. It draws a sword in the face of the familiar—the beloved—the man's own family. He is left to choose. This choice, however, offers hope.*

*The choice is not between freedom and bondage, hope and despair, or contentment and want. He has already chosen life. In Christ he has already gained freedom, been granted hope, and seized upon that which makes man content. He must choose between self and God. His choice is this: Is God's Word truth or fiction? Once this is settled in a man's soul, there is no authority or devil that can build a wall big enough to keep that man from **approaching** God and gaining access by faith to all that belongs to the heirs of God's Kingdom. An intimate, breathtaking, romantic*

relationship with God is available to all that know Him.
If you desire intimacy with God, it's yours for the taking,
*albeit at great cost. Worship is costly, therefore **approach** is*
dangerous—never calculated, yet of untold reward.

THE TOUCHSTONE OF APPROACH

That's the theme of this chapter, and in my opinion, the key theme of the entire book. So let's get to the main point—how do we approach God? My emphasis here will be on studying *your* approach to God, not admiring and replicating *my* approach to God. Unfortunately, we have the tendency in the body of Christ to read a book and turn the principles taught into a method sought. We package the truth and sell it as a proven formula for success. An intimate relationship with God can never be boiled down to a learned task. God does not submit to our attempts, even unaware, of subtle manipulation.

Let's not look to a method. Take a look at your own personal approach to God. Be willing to adjust or change it. *If you are not confident in your approach to God, you will lack intimacy with Him.* How do you approach God? What is your relationship with God like? Why do I ask? Because your approach to God is going to affect what your relationship with God will be.

I remember one of my very first summer jobs. I worked at a concession stand at a baseball diamond. My job duties included making popcorn, stocking the coolers, and working the sales counter during games. During one encounter with a customer, I hesitated about the decision I had to make. I froze up, as they would say. One of my co-workers, an adult volunteer, noticed my moment of indecision, and decided to step in. He took the item I was holding out of my hands, walked up to the counter, and finished the transaction with the customer. Then he turned to me with a look of displeasure on his face and said, "He who hesitates is lost." He wasn't joking; he was serious.

There was no intention on his part to encourage, shed some light upon the situation, or show the least bit of kindness. It was definitely not the way to deal with a fifteen-year-old just joining the workforce.

What do you think my approach to this man was like the rest of the summer? I certainly stayed away from him. I didn't want to work at the same time he did. If this minute example, from a seemingly harmless experience, had such a great affect on my approach towards this man, how much more does the entire weight of our life experiences affect our approach to God?

WAITING TO EXHALE

I recently purchased a new car. Well, it's actually six years old, but it sure has the feel of new. I'm sure you have experienced what I am feeling right now. Like a child with a new toy, my enthusiasm is high. I just want to tinker with it and drive it around town. However, along with the joy and satisfaction that owning a new car brings, I find myself full of hesitation. My joy is tempered not by a lack of confidence in the decision I made, but for another important reason. What if the engine in my new vehicle blows? What if the transmission goes out next week? Then I didn't get as good of a deal as I thought. I start to wonder if I could have bought a similar car for less money. So I find myself looking in the newspaper at the vehicles for sale, just to assure myself that I got a good deal. In my mind I walk on eggshells, not because of the truth, but because of what could be the truth in the future.

Do you think I am just acting silly? Probably, but why do you and I do the same thing in something that really matters—our relationship with God? There is a hesitation in our approach to God. We hold our breath, waiting to exhale. Sometimes it's subtle, at other times quite obvious. I doubt that it's fear of the unknown that holds us back. Yet a feeling of uneasiness comes over us and keeps us at a distance from the very God who beckons us to draw near. We find ourselves acting like a student called to the principal's office. Have you ever been called to the boss's office, only to walk in and see the human resources representative sitting there as well? Unfortunately, that's exactly what some people envision approaching God to be like.

It's often easy to see this hesitation manifested in others. When I pray with someone, for instance, my heart observes their approach to God. At times I wonder, what just happened to this friend or acquaintance of mine? They were talking to me like they felt comfortable with me, like they would with any friend. Then they switch their attention to God as they start to pray, and something changes. There is an obvious change in the tone of their voice. Awkwardness sets in, like the feeling of not knowing what to say. Finally, after stumbling through a few sentences, they finish their prayer in a state of mid-thought.

Is such behavior simply a result of the fear of speaking in public? Is it a reflection of believers not knowing how to pray? I don't think either is correct. **God's people show a reluctance to exhale in His presence.** It's indicative of something much greater than mere hesitation, or a lack of knowledge concerning prayer. It reveals a lack of intimacy with the one we call our Lover. We have one style of approach that we use in relationships with each other, and a totally different approach that we use with God.

Is there a deep longing in your soul to fully exhale in the presence of God? You can be completely relaxed and at rest as you approach Him. Imagine yourself with no hesitation, no need to "dress up", and all your cares are laid aside. *Whatever cares you have as you stand at the door, you take and cast upon the Lord. Then you walk right through that door and enter into His presence. You approach with every burden lifted, every yoke broken, and all fears held in disregard. This is what it means to exhale in His presence. And the more it becomes a habit in your life, the easier and more enjoyable your approach to God will become.*

These are the themes I want to focus on as it relates to the concept of approach: 1) Approach in faith. 2) Approach in freedom. 3) Approach with confidence.

Approach in Faith

There is no limit to your experience of intimacy because of faith. The road to intimacy is long, but faith steers the way. Intimacy fills and refreshes the Christian voyager along this tiresome road of faith. Faith makes it possible to hope. Faith's reach is determined by man, measured by God, and limited by man. There are no dead-end streets on the road of faith. There is no end game. There is no final mountain to climb. It has no limit, lest God be small. Faith's resources are never wasted, never vanquished, forever fruitful. The pleasing of God begins with faith, continues by faith, and ends with faith; otherwise, God is simply not pleased. (Heb. 10:38) Therefore we must learn how to approach God in faith.

If faith were merely a wish upon a star, it would be cute. But it is supernatural truth, not just an unexplainable phenomenon—truth! *The human mind cannot fathom it; the doubter cannot grasp it; and the manipulator cannot possess it. It stands apart in its beauty—designed by God.* Keep in mind that unless you are walking in love with others, your faith will mean nothing. (1Cor. 13:2) In fact, "The only thing that counts is faith expressing itself through love." (Gal. 5:6b)

So how do you and I respond to this challenge of faith? Unfortunately, we have a highly predictable response. It's all too often mechanical, programmed, lifeless, and performance-oriented. Oh, it's genuine and sincere. Upon coming to know Him, we sincerely raise the bar. Of course we can never seem to hurdle it. It's like the low bar of "limbo", which no one is ever able to duck under. We just keep trying harder, and it only adds to our frustration. How quickly we forget grace.

Some treat faith as a special event. In this case, it is <u>used</u> to obtain a desired result, or <u>exercised</u> in dire circumstances. Nonetheless, it has been designed by God to be our way of life. "For in him we live and move and have our being." (Acts 17:28) This cannot be accomplished without faith. We can't move in Him unless we are pleasing Him. "And without faith it is impossible to please God, because anyone who comes to him must believe that he exists and that he rewards those who earnestly seek him." (Heb. 11:6) Just as it is possible to fail grace (Heb. 12:15), we often fail faith and seldom realize it. One way that we do this is by robbing God of His pleasure. How do we do that? We do it by choosing to live in fear and doubt. When we walk in faith, God takes pleasure and is pleased. By choosing to fail faith (yes, it is a choice), we choose to rob God of the sweet aroma that is due His glory.

By now we see the importance of faith, and we desire intimacy with God. So let's move on. How do we approach God in faith? What does that look like? Let's keep it simple. I'm just simple enough to believe God, and I have the audacity to believe that God is faithful to what He has promised to be. That's faith—that's how you approach God. We just read it in Hebrews 11:6. We must approach God believing that He rewards those who earnestly seek Him. Faith is confidence; it is assurance. *Approaching God in faith means that we know that He hears us and has granted what we asked of Him.* "This is the confidence we have in approaching God: that if we ask anything according to his will, he hears us. And if we know that he hears us—whatever we ask—we know that we have what we asked of him." (1 John 5:14-15)

APPROACH IN FREEDOM

Living and experiencing a life of freedom is far different from being told that you are free. Even when you believe it, you still need to take it to the next level. You can see how important freedom is to God in the Bible. Christ set us free from the bondage of sin so that we could walk in freedom. "It is for freedom that Christ has set us free." (Gal. 5:1) "You, my brothers, were called to be free." (Gal. 5:13) *What does it accomplish in us when we approach God in freedom? We experience God in a way that we never could if we were living bound by legalism or burdened by the cares of this world. Simply put, we can't experience the God who dwells in freedom if we don't approach Him in freedom.*

41

What does it mean to be free? What does true freedom look like? We can't talk about approaching God in freedom without talking about children. I sometimes hesitate to make the connection because of my concern that people won't be able to relate to the life of a child. We look at children and tend to think, "That's nice; that's so sweet. But my life is so far removed from the world that a child lives in." If a child lived in your world, what would they be like? *We can't fit your world into the life of a child—but you can put on the likeness of a child and we can put you back into your world as a new person. Then you can experience life in a new way. Moreover, you can experience God in a new way.*

To force your world on a little child would be awkward, burdensome, of no use. For young children, it's not a matter of being able to understand your world or possessing the capacity to deal with adult issues. That is obviously missing in a child. But children possess something far more valuable than that. They have the capacity to approach everything in life in a state of innocence. The heart and mind of a young child were created by God to be innocent of the clutter that darkens your world. Here's the clutter: fear, worry, stress, restlessness, shame, anxiety, lust, and anger. Throw in painful memories of the past, the heartache of failed relationships, financial loss, career disappointment, and loneliness—now that's a world our children don't need and can do without ever experiencing. *You can bring a child into your world, but they will continue to live as though they belong to a different one. And so must we. That's how we approach God in freedom—like we belong to a different world.*

If we don't approach in freedom, our relationship with God will become legalistic and ritualistic. It will become dead religion, merely going through the motions. Boldness and freedom, especially these two, declares that you know God well. You know Him, that's why you approach Him that way. Freedom is a dance; it's a decree. It says, "Even if the whole world is watching—I don't really care. I've found my treasure, and I'm free to delight in Him—anywhere and anytime."

To approach God in freedom is to know you are free. What does that do for you—to be set free? Now you are free to live, free to dance, free to love others. How does that come about? It happens when you know you are free, and you have a heart full of gratitude toward the Lord for it. You realize the depths to which you have been set free and forgiven. You "allow yourself" to be free as you dance in freedom by receiving and embracing these truths. By "letting yourself off the hook", you let go of the burdens you were never meant to bear. You choose to exercise the rights that are only granted to members of royalty. Only sons and daughters of the King are allowed to dance in His presence in the throne room. And that's who you are. Like the woman in Luke 7:47, you live and love in a new way because you realize how much God has forgiven you. Jesus said, "I tell you that her many sins are forgiven. This is clear, because she showed great love. People who are forgiven only a little will love only a little." (ERV)

To approach God in freedom is to worship like no one is watching, at home, church—wherever you are. You approach like a child. Sometimes you skip, sometimes you dance, and sometimes you run. At times you just dive into His arms and put your head on His chest. But you always approach like a son or daughter who knows they belong there, especially when you don't feel like you do. When everything inside of you, and every voice outside, tells you that you don't—that's when you dance in freedom before the Lord. That's freedom my friends; it pleases God. Exercising that freedom will take a lot of confidence.

APPROACH WITH CONFIDENCE

We will discuss confidence again in chapter seven when we talk about the keys to intimacy with God. Right now I want to discuss it as it relates to, and helps to define, the concept of approach.

Do you feel a lack of confidence when you approach God? We know that confidence is built, little by little. Thank God, we know that confidence can be regained once lost. If confidence is indeed built one small step at a time, then how is it attained? And if we are in need of regaining or growing in it, then where do we start? Is it different for every set of circumstances in life (i.e. relationships, marketplace, and education)? While it is unique to these various circumstances, the foundation of confidence is always the same. So let's start at the beginning. We start with the faith of a child, believing God. We grow in confidence through practice, in this case practicing the presence of God. *Confidence is attained as the small steps produce roots that grow deep, anchoring our souls in hope.*

Why do we need to approach God with confidence? Let's go one step further—let's say boldness. Why would any child of God walk into His presence with boldness? Because you know Him; you know what pleases Him. You know you belong there, and you know who you are in Christ. God tells us in the Bible why we need confidence. "Dear friends, if our hearts do not condemn us, we have confidence before God and receive from him anything we ask; because we obey his commands and do what pleases him." (1John 3:21-22) Do you want to receive from God? It's not all up to God! We have a big part in this. A lack of confidence will keep us from what God has for us.

The second reason we are to approach with confidence is because it gives God pleasure. What's the opposite of confidence? That would be shrinking back, wavering, being double-minded, and unsure. What does that do to our relationship with God? It robs the Lord of the pleasure He desires. Am I being too strong? Read it for yourself:

> **So do not throw away your confidence; it will be richly rewarded.** You need to persevere so that when you have done the will of God, you will receive what he has promised. For in just a very little while, 'He who is coming will come and will not delay. But my righteous one will live by faith. **And if he shrinks back, I will not be pleased with him.**' But we are not of those who shrink back and are destroyed, but of those who believe and are saved. (Heb. 10:35-39)

Verse 38 in the King James Version reads, "Now the just shall live by faith: but if any man draw back, **my soul shall have no pleasure in him**." This is God speaking. He's telling us that He gets no pleasure in seeing His children shrink back because of a lack of confidence. We were created to give pleasure to the Creator. "Thou art worthy, O Lord, to receive glory and honor and power: for thou hast created all things, and for thy pleasure they are and were created." (Rev. 4:11 KJV)

What does this approach with confidence do for us? It makes us bold as a lion. We walk into God's presence with our heads held high, not dragging our feet with our heads cast down in defeat. We come to God in prayer without shame, condemnation, guilt, or fear. We then believe that God wants us there. He loves us. He's not mad at us. Confidence helps us believe that God has a plan for each one of us—and it's a good plan! Confidence gives us hope that God is going to work something good in our lives. Confidence doesn't negate humility—it strengthens it!

I'm sure you are comfortable in the confines of your own home. It's probably the place that all of us feel the most relaxed. How about at your best friend's house? How do you act there? Let's take a trip to the house of one of my best friends. Here we go.

I'm knocking on the door. He's home—but occupied. He can't come to the door right now. (He yells to me from somewhere in the house) "Scott, come in." I don't hesitate. I open the door and walk in. (He yells again) "Hey Scott, I'm busy with something. I've got to finish this. Give me a few minutes. Make yourself at home."

I do exactly what my friend told me to do. I act like I'm at my own house. I open the fridge to see what's in there to drink. If I see something I like, I grab it. I see a bag of chips on the kitchen counter; I help myself. I grab the remote—turn on the television. Lying down on the couch, I start flicking through the channels. Finally, my friend makes his way to the living room to greet me. He laughs and says, "Good, that's what I would have wanted you to do."

When a friend comes to my house, I treat him the same. It doesn't matter what I have going on. The door is always open. I don't care if I am eating Thanksgiving dinner with my family. My response is always the same—"Come on in. Grab a plate. Join us at the dinner table."

Now try to personalize this as if I was talking to you, and you are one of my friends. What happens when I tell you these things, but you don't believe them? I sense you feel uneasy about my invitation. I've told you many times, but it's obvious you still don't feel comfortable doing it. What am I to conclude from your lack of response to my invitation? I conclude that: a) you're not comfortable with my invitation; b) you're not comfortable in my presence; or c) you really don't believe me.

When you are comfortable in God's presence, it shows. It shows up in worship, prayer, and your desire toward God. Like the journey we just took to my friend's house, you find yourself able to relax in the presence of God. You make yourself at home—because in fact—you are at home.

In Paul's letter to the Ephesians we read:

> But God, being rich in mercy, because of His great love with which He loved us, even when we were dead in our transgressions, made us alive together with Christ (by grace you have been saved), and raised us up with Him, and **seated us with Him in the heavenly places in Christ Jesus**, so that in the ages to come He might show the surpassing riches of His grace in kindness toward us in Christ Jesus. (Eph. 2:4-7 NASB)

What does this mean? It means a number of things. It tells us what our position is with God spiritually. And it tells us in past tense, meaning that it has already been done for us. It points to a position of strength, security, and authority that God has given to us, His children.

Yet it implies something else that I would like to expound upon. John Dawson, author of the book <u>The Father Heart of God</u>, says that being seated with Christ in heavenly places implies three things. It implies relaxation, acceptance, and belonging. What do relaxation, acceptance, and belonging have to do with intimacy? Your most intimate relationships are going to be the ones where you can be yourself, let down your hair so to speak, and still be accepted. If you have an intimate relationship with those in your home, you are able to fully relax. You are confident you belong there. It's no different with God.

Next we are going to take a look at our personal view of God, and how it was formed. The importance of the next chapter cannot be overstated, only for the fact that our view of God greatly influences our approach to God. Now that we have established how important our approach to God is, we need to take a serious look at our view of Him, so we can make the necessary changes to experience intimacy.

CHAPTER 5

Understanding How We Relate to God

Satan promised Adam and Eve an experiential knowledge of "good and evil". With this experience, man, now left to himself, would be able to distinguish good and evil on his own—or so the serpent implied. Since man is his own god, he is free to write his own rules.

*We have already learned that the serpent was quite right in this respect: Disobedience did give Adam and Eve a new knowledge of evil. They did not merely know evil abstractly as a concept of the mind, but as the probing of a restless conscience. From that point on, their moral perception was clouded as **they struggled with the need to reconcile their lifestyle with the image of God, which had been defaced but not erased from their minds and hearts.***

The problem, of course, is that in their fallen state they could never again perceive good and evil as God saw it. If left to themselves, they would have to build their own system of conduct with the fragmentary knowledge of their own sinful perceptions and tainted conscience. What is more, they would discover that they could not live up to what they intuitively knew to be right. Simply put, they would have to become relativists, giving up all hope of finding a unified system of morality and truth.[5]

Even today as believers, we are tempted to look at the world and believe that we have been shortchanged. It is not just teenagers who often think to themselves, "If only I weren't a Christian, think of all the fun things I could do!" Thus, while others enjoy the pleasures of sin, we, poor creatures that we are, must stay at home and be content with the limitless wonders of God's matchless grace. Thus the sons of the King of kings feel sorry for themselves![6]

FORMING OUR VIEW OF GOD

*A*s we just read in the quote by Lutzer, there are many who struggle with the need to reconcile their lifestyle with the image of God. They make it more difficult for themselves by having a faulty view of God. *We don't struggle with God as much as we struggle with our own concepts of who God is. Seldom do we allow anyone to enter into the room where we keep our concepts of God. That is hallowed ground. That is a secret place; a place where no visitors are allowed. It is off limits to the general public.*

Our concepts of God are much easier to embrace than the reality of God Himself. Therefore we do not like to question the concepts we have created. Yet one cannot become intimate, or dance, with a mere concept. For the very nature of God confronts the concepts we cling to, and threatens the foundation we have built our lives upon. We must confront them, however, for change to occur in our lives.

All we truly long for in life: love, freedom, relationship, joy, and peace, can only be obtained when we see God for who He really is. It

---

5   Erwin W. Lutzer, *The Serpent of Paradise* (Chicago: Moody Press, 1996), 61-62.

6   Ibid., 44.

is obtained through the experiencing of His reality in our daily life. To behold such beauty and come to the knowledge of such truth is to be set free, to be released from years of bondage to fear. To live in the truth of that hope will change our lives forever. Our old concepts must leave. In confronting our concepts we have crucified our past. Now we can approach God in a new way. Then the intimacy we long for can begin to develop.

Our approach to God is dependent on how we relate to Him. We find ourselves relating to Him based upon the view of God we have formed. This is the order—forming our view of God—relating to a specific aspect of His character—approaching Him. It all begins with our personal view of God. So let's begin there.

Our view of God is quite complicated actually. There are several factors involved in shaping it. *Once you begin to understand how you picture God, you'll understand why you relate to Him as you do. Before we crack open the pages of the Bible for the very first time, or utter those first words of prayer, we have already decided in our minds who we think God is.* Every man has their own view of Him, whether they are a believer or not. So when someone commits their life to Jesus and becomes saved, they are already bringing this view into the picture. Often unaware, they have brought their views of God from the past into the present reality where they now stand. That's why the ABC's of Christian growth I wrote about in chapter 3 are simply not enough for the disciple. We must discover what our view of God is and how it was formed. Then we must address the faulty concepts that fed this view. Finally, with the Holy Spirit's help, we shape it into a view that is biblical and honoring to God.

Go to your local Christian bookstore and take a look around. You'll find at least half a dozen different pictures of Jesus on assorted cards, plaques, and framed art. Which of the portraits are correct? Don't be surprised if the answer is none. It's impossible of course to know what the face of Jesus actually looks like, for now at least. That lack of knowledge, however, hasn't stopped us from creating our own opinions.

Those opinions range from the Jesus with the solemn face, to the Jesus with the beaming smile. I personally like the picture of Jesus playing with children along the pathway, His face bursting with jubilant laughter. Have you seen that one? I'm not sure if that portrait exists on canvas, but it sure exists in my mind! Of course our portrait would not be complete without the shoulder length hair, the neatly trimmed beard, and those deep-piercing eyes. Oh, did I forget the gown? Some still like to picture Him with short hair and beardless, although somehow those long locks of hair just seem perfect for Jesus, no matter what generation your opinion comes from.

Of course it is not a mere physical view of God I am speaking of. Neither is it simply the ability to visualize God that I write about. *Our view of God is our belief in His character and how He interacts with each of His own children.* It is formed over many years by several unique influences. Furthermore, these influences on our life have numerous sources. Let's take a look at some of the major influences on the formation of our personal view of God.

No matter what you picture God to be like, it is very likely that you came to that conclusion through one of three ways: 1) your relationships with authority figures; 2) education (past and present); or 3) the influence of a particular individual. Hence, we can't simply ignore these facts; we must address them. When we say, "just read the Bible if you want to know who God is", or "just pray about it", we give an exiguous answer. Of course the Bible is the authority and place where we will find out who God is—absolutely! There really isn't anywhere else you should look. Yet the reason why this answer just isn't good enough is because we bring so many preconceived ideas into the process. The ideas become concepts that govern the way we relate to God. The concepts are usually learned in early childhood, and then developed throughout our entire adult lives. It is these concepts that we must deal with. Once we have laid the foundation with a proper perspective of who God is, based on scripture, we can move on toward maturity. That maturity will only become a reality as we deal with the wrong foundational perceptions about God that we continue to cling to.

AUTHORITY FIGURES

This is the area of greatest influence and impact. The other two areas of influence (education, and the influence of a particular individual) pale in comparison to this one. While they are very important, especially the positive impact of a particular individual, the damage caused by authority figures tends to overshadow everything else. Because of this, we will devote most of our time to analyzing the impact it has on us. I want to emphasize that I am not advocating that we obtain our concept of God from a man or woman in authority. Not surprisingly, we see many aspects of God's character lived out in the life of His servants here on earth. But after all, that is what Christianity is all about—the followers of Christ reflecting His image to a dying world. The problem occurs when we form our concept of God from our past relationships with authority, and then fail to correct them once we are introduced to the Word of God.

Many relate to God as they have related to authority figures throughout their entire lives. The authority figures are usually parents, policemen, politicians, teachers, clergy, or former employers. *These relationships have a tremendous impact on the early formation of your concept of God. You will find that those early concepts, which seem imbedded in your mind at times, are very difficult to uproot.* Yet why are they so deeply imbedded? Let's look deeper into the impact.

It was never God's intention for man to be ruled by any king, other than Himself.

> But when they said, 'Give us a king to lead us,' this
> displeased Samuel; so he prayed to the Lord. And the Lord
> told him: 'Listen to all that the people are saying to you;

it is not you they have rejected, but they have rejected me as their king. As they have done from the day I brought them up out of Egypt until this day, forsaking me and serving other gods, so they are doing to you. Now listen to them; but warn them solemnly and let them know what the king who will reign over them will do.' Samuel told all the words of the Lord to the people who were asking him for a king. He said, 'this is what the king who will reign over you will do: He will take your sons... He will take your daughters... He will take the best of your fields... He will take a tenth of your flocks, and you yourselves will become his slaves. When that day comes, you will cry out for relief from the king you have chosen, and the Lord will not answer you in that day.' (1Sam. 8:6-18)

God, through His omniscient wisdom, foresaw the problems we would have. He knew that men would misrepresent Him. And because of this misrepresentation of authority, men would therefore be turned off to God. Hence, we have a problem when we form our concept of who God is from the view that we are given by imperfect authority. Men will ultimately fail us. There is no way that any man can portray God as clearly as He is portrayed in scripture. However, knowing this has not stopped us from holding those in authority to the same standard we hold God.

Let's look at how this attraction to the authority figures in our life begins. It all starts at an early age. Our first encounter with authority occurs during childhood. It occurs on the day of our birth, to be exact. If we were to get technical, the first contact we have with an authority figure in our life is not our parents, but the doctor who delivers us! There you are in that nice warm environment of your mother's womb, when all of a sudden something clasps onto your head and starts dragging you out. It's the doctor, and you don't have much of a say in this whole process. It's your first brush with authority! And when you arrive on the scene you voice your opposition loudly.

Hopefully your birth went a little easier than that rude awakening I just described. Maybe you slid into a warm pool of water. Anyway, here you are. Now it's time to meet your next authority figure—your parents. **It is they who will hold the key to your view of God during the formative years of your life.**

And form you they shall. You quickly learn that they are the boss around the house. The impact your parents have on you is cyclopean. Not only do they feed, clothe, and bathe you, they do something even more significant. They teach you. Mom and dad are your first role models. You will spend your early childhood years observing their actions, mirroring their personality. The optimum challenge for you at this young age is to imitate the way they talk, walk, eat, and laugh. The challenge for your parents is to teach you more than basic survival in the realm of life. They must lay a spiritual foundation for you; a straight and narrow course that one day will guide you to your own personal relationship with the Creator of the universe, the Lover of your soul.

Although all parents don't share this desire to lay a spiritual foundation for their children, they all become a part of God's plan. They may not even believe in God. Yet, God uses them to reveal Himself to you. Whether they realize it or not, your parents are demonstrating to you the first attribute of God's character you will encounter in life—unconditional love.

I believe the child who comes to this realization will not only have a positive self concept, they will have formed an opinion about God that is positive as well. There are exceptions to this naturally. The child may have been raised in a loving home, but may never have been told about the love of God. I have met people who have had a very positive childhood life, and can attest to the fact that their parents were loving role models for them, but have no concept of God. They simply were never taught about Him.

We encounter many other authority figures before we leave our parents' home, most notably teachers. And the association doesn't stop there. Once we leave we will encounter the employer, the landlord, and the tax collector. Each will have an impact on our life, although none will be greater than our parents' impact. We aspire to some of the benefits that go along with holding a place of authority, such as respect, admiration, power, and the feeling that what you do is significant. Perhaps the aspect of *attraction* to authority figures in our life is greatest when we look at the impact teachers have on us. Often they are the means by which we learn respect outside of our own home.

If our parents and teachers had a positive impact on our upbringing, you would think that the authority figures in our lives presented us with an excellent opportunity to develop a healthy concept of who God is. Maybe that is the case with you. Ask yourself this question: What authority figure has had the greatest impact, positive or negative, on the concept of God I now believe?

If you became a Christian as an adult, it is possible that you would point to your pastor as having the greatest influence on the development of your concept of God. Once again, we are not trying to replace the Bible as the source of truth for forming those concepts. We are asserting the fact that man, in the role of an authority figure, has been one of the ways through which we have come to think the way we do about God.

I don't believe we ever expect mere men to fully represent God Himself.

But they are the only examples we have of authority figures here on earth. We know that God is an authority figure; He is the highest authority, to be exact. So isn't it natural for us to think that God must deal with us just as they do? If we had a past experience with tyrannical authority figures, and most of us have, wouldn't we be prone to equating their actions with that of God's? This would be true especially before we come to Christ. We have no other examples to draw from up to this point in our lives. So we convince ourselves that we have a very good reason to believe as we do.

How much has our past experience with authority affected who we are today? It probably has affected us much more than we realize or would admit to. Maybe our experience went like this: An authority figure failed us. It was mainly our parents' fault. They were too performance-driven. Our fathers were never involved with our growing up. They never spent much time with us. And when they did, we were led to believe that what we do will always be more important than who we are. Then there was that teacher in junior high—she only reinforced that idea. How about that run-in with the law? No grace was shown there, only a stiff fine and a lecture from the judge. That politician promised he would lower our taxes! And how about the layoff we suffered right before Christmas?

These examples are very real, sincere, and considerably common, unfortunately. They are legitimate excuses for the past, and they have affected the way we currently think. Each of us approaches God in a different way, based on many factors. As you can see, this whole area of authority figures is a major factor in determining the way we approach God today. But now we have become that new creation in Christ. (2Cor. 5:17) So we are to "put off our old self...be made new in the attitude of our minds; and to put on the new self, created to be like God..." (Eph. 4:22-24) That's going to take some time. We need to heal from the wounds of past experience. Trust needs to be built; faith needs to grow. Then we can learn to approach God in a new way, in confidence.

HOW WE RELATE TO GOD

Let's face it—we are relational beings. God created us that way, for relationship with Himself and others. We are also sensual beings, that is, we are devoted to the pleasures of the senses (think in terms of purity here). The Creator gave us these senses, and it is simply our way of assimilating life. That's why we form pictures in our minds of who God is. *Since we are sensual beings who desire relationship, we feel a strong need to see, touch, hear, smell, and taste God for ourselves. It is* no wonder then that the role of our soul (mind, will, and emotions) is so prevalent in the specific way that you and I relate to God.

There are five main aspects of God's character. We relate to Jesus as our <u>Savior</u>. We relate to God as our <u>Father</u>. We submit to Him as <u>Lord</u>. We know Him as a close <u>Friend</u>. And finally, as the bride of Christ we call Him our <u>Lover</u>.

All of us identify with one aspect of God's character as our primary focus in relating to Him, whenever we visualize or conceptualize who He is. Some identify easily with Jesus as their personal friend, but struggle with the role He wants to take as Lord over every area of their lives. Therefore their approach to God will consistently deal with Him in the particular aspect that they feel most comfortable with, in this case, as friend. We can't focus all of our attention on one or two of His attributes, however, while we totally ignore the others. This produces a lopsided, unhealthy, and immature relationship with God. Some of us may feel uncomfortable approaching God as our lover. Others, because of their relationship, or lack thereof, with their earthly fathers, have a hard time relating to God as their loving Father. And finally, there are some believers who never relate to God as their friend, because they can't picture Him as a friend; they don't believe it's possible for a holy God to have a friendship with man.

While each of us relates to one or two of God's attributes more so than the others, this often changes according to what we think our needs are at the present time. For instance, if you see yourself predominantly as a sinner, or simply in need of repentance today, you will relate to the corresponding role of God to meet that specific need (Savior). *As we grow in being sensitive to God's Spirit, and allow Him to lead as we dance together, the change will be according to what He thinks our needs are, not what we think.* We need to be careful not to place the emphasis of our relationship on ourselves. I felt it important here to recognize the fact that we often approach God with our minds on our own need. But it is still that overriding view of God that each of us has that determines what our approach to Him will be.

How often have you approached God in prayer about a specific need, only to finish that prayer time with your mind and heart focused on a totally different thing? Let's say you are praying earnestly for a job, or God's immediate financial provision. It has been consuming your thoughts. Most of your time with God is spent petitioning Him for this great need you have. You need to experience His salvation, so you approach Him in the role of Savior. You are also looking to God in His role as Father, as you know it is His will to give good things to His children.

Then one day in prayer, the Holy Spirit begins to remind you of God's faithfulness. He shows you His goodness and gives you hope that you will soon see His kindness poured out on your life, just as you have seen before. Soon you find yourself praising Him. He reminds you of how good He has been to you in the past, and your heart is flooded with worship. The next few days are spent in praise. Perhaps you enter into a period of repentance; you repent of your lack of worship, thanksgiving, and gratitude for God's kindness. You begin to approach God as your Lover. Before you know it, you are caught up in dancing with God. You have completely forgotten about your present needs, and you are overwhelmed with a sense of intimacy that is building between you and your lover—God.

What's happening here? Your view of God has changed by the promptings of the Holy Spirit. Your approach to God in prayer is different now. You are relating to Him in a new way. The change does not occur because of the attention you have given to your need. It occurs because of the awareness of who God is, through this intimate encounter with Him. As you gain a proper view of who He is, you will never approach Him in the same way again. Take a look at Job 42:5-6. Many think that Job was changed because of what he endured in trials. Guess again my friend. He received a glimpse of God. And that glimpse was enough to shake him to the core. Job said, "**My ears had heard of you but now my eyes have seen you. Therefore I despise myself** and repent in dust and ashes."

Job's approach to God changed for the rest of his life. First, his view changed (verse 5). Then he repented of everything that had to do with himself, and began to relate to God in newness of life. He actually despised himself! Job wasn't saying, "I despise the way I spend my time and my money. I've wasted my life here on this earth." No, he went much further. In light of this new view of God he had received, Job wanted nothing to do with his old life anymore. He didn't care to know or discover the inner voice inside Job. He wasn't merely weeping because he had lost everything. He wept with tears of repentance because he had seen the Lord, and everything else in life became vanity to him!

Job's friends were rebuked by God because they had a flawed view of God, and it came out in what they said. It influenced their injurious advice to Job. (Job 42:7) But God commended Job because he had a proper view of the Almighty, and he spoke rightly about God. (Job 42:8) Our view of God will affect how we relate to Him, and our approach to Him, and therefore affect whether we are pleasing God or not.

CHAPTER 6

The Five Keys to Intimacy with God

KEY #1—BECOME LIKE A CHILD

Beneath the layers of understanding lies a key so small, yet so significant, it can only have meaning when left untouched. It cannot be grasped or obtained through perception. Its beauty is felt in its simplicity, its strength in utter dependence.

The wisdom of her teachings is learned in naivety. Her gentle allurement is universal. Yet she refuses to be contained. Her laughter is as natural as rivers of water. Freedom is her outer garment, peace and joy—the wellspring of her soul.

The man who seeks understanding alone—he knows not her dwelling place. She can only be found by the man who seeks God. This man finds wisdom. This man knows the home of understanding. It's a home that is only found in the secret place, a path with one start and end point—the presence of the Living God.

Key#1 to Intimacy: Become like a child. Key#2: Simplify your life. Key#3: Approach God with confidence. Key#4: Discover your beauty to God. Key#5: Delight yourself in the Lord.

You need to become like a child. We've all heard this before. Yet, what does it mean? Our very salvation starts with this. Jesus said, "I tell you the truth, anyone who will not receive the kingdom of God like a little child will never enter it." (Luke 18:17) Not only does His kingdom need to be received with a childlike faith, it needs to be perceived with one as well. "At that time Jesus said, 'I praise you, Father, Lord of heaven and earth, because you have hidden these things from the wise and learned, and revealed them to little children. Yes, Father, for this was your good pleasure.'" (Matt. 11:25-26)

I think most believers have a basic grasp of this concept. If you were to ask Joe Christian, he would tell you that we need to have the faith of a child as we trust God in childlike innocence. *The problem is that we tend to only associate this concept with salvation, and therefore miss out on the rest of the story. Even with the understanding we have as adults, we tend to look at childhood through a window. As our eyes are pressed against the plane of glass, we watch with fascination and longing. We admire their beauty, yet falsely assume that we no longer can enter the room to become as one of them.* If you have a problem seeing yourself as a child, and just as important—approaching God as a child—you might struggle with the rest of this chapter.

To become like a child involves three things: #1 The Restoration of Innocence; #2 The Resolution of Freedom; #3 The Resilience of Faith. We will start with the only entry point to understanding this topic—the restoration of innocence.

THE RESTORATION OF INNOCENCE

The wonderment of life itself is found in the simplicity of innocence. So when we lose innocence, we lose life; or at the very least, we lose the ability to see with the Creator's eyes, think with the Creator's mind, touch with the Creator's hands, and feel with the Creator's heart. No measure of significance can be placed on a matter so weighty. The loss of innocence opens one's soul to the brutality of life, the dark side of reality.

We don't know what to do with this thing called life. We can't handle really living. A pseudo lifestyle is developed and embraced by many, in the hope of escaping the realities that each day brings to our doorstep. Hence the attraction we have to such things as television, internet, and dream vacations. They offer us an escape; an opportunity to stand on the outside of our reality and pretend it does not exist.

Life comes with a suitcase full of baggage. We don't like to think about the contents of that suitcase, so we store it away in a place that will allow us to seldom be reminded of it. If you want life you must accept all that comes with it—failure, rejection, loss, pain, and yes—death. The end result is the ruination of all that was once precious and innocent. *Even those two words—precious and innocent—are reserved for very few. We attach their meaning primarily to children. It's not a matter of searching to find something in life that embodies their true meaning. Our minds quickly run to the image of a child. The problem is—that child we see in our minds is never us.* Our vision needs to be upgraded. If we can, as adult believers, see ourselves as precious and innocent, we can begin to approach God and all of life with a childlike faith. How does one upgrade their vision? Start by changing what you believe; add to it how you think; finish with how you see.

Children live their lives with different eyes. There is no suitcase full of baggage. They quickly forget pain and rejection; they bounce off of failure. Their limitations in knowledge and maturity are overpowered by zeal, freedom, and purity. Fear becomes a wall for most of us, dictating much of our interactions with others (whether we are aware of it or not). For the young child, fear simply has a different meaning. It is a choice, not an adopted way of life, like it is with many adults who use it as a defense mechanism. For the most part, fear has not laid a foundation in the life of a young child, therefore there is incredible freedom. For the adult, brick upon brick is laid over the course of a lifetime of experiences, until there is finally a wall—a daunting task to climb.

Young children approach life in a way that is vastly dissimilar to the way you and I approach it. Each day for them is fresh, seemingly disconnected from the previous day. A child is "just along for the ride", as the saying goes. They have no choice; they sit in the passenger seat. Their lives succumb to the will of the driver of the vehicle— their parents. Perhaps that's why as adults, we find the course of our lives to often be frustrating, because being "just along for the ride" has much greater implications. We find it hard, as believers, to take our hands off the steering wheel and allow God to lead. Some have been down a road full of potholes and detours, and quite frankly, are not happy with the driver of the vehicle. Others are not even aware of the fact that they have been driving their own vehicle for so long. They have failed to notice the owner of the vehicle, Jesus Christ, is in the back seat weeping. If this is you, repent before God now, and become like a child again in your relationship with Him.

Am I saying that you can approach each day as carefree as a child, even though you have the maturity of an adult? Absolutely! Could each day be like a fresh start? Yes! To many, this sounds too good to be true. And yet, you and I have longed for this kind of life for years. It is possible. "All things are possible to him who believes." (Mark 9:23 NASB)

Many years ago, when my children were very young, I was in a conversation with them concerning their freedom to do a certain activity. I sensed an opportunity to talk with them about the dangers facing them in the world, and the need for my wife and I to protect them. I explained that we needed to keep an eye on them because someone could take them. I could see the wheels in their innocent minds moving as they tried to digest this. Finally, our daughter Victoria spoke up, "Daddy, why would anyone want to take us?" Had Adam and Eve never sinned, none of us would have needed to ever initiate this conversation with our children. We have strayed far from this innocence, but it can be restored.

Are you ready to go a little deeper? Let's think about this process of restoration. Imagine life without fear or worry. Imagine every day as a new adventure. Can you imagine not having the scars of the past that mark our lives? How would we live our lives today if these things were true? We would live life like never before. But how do we start? First, we'll look at how children approach life, and then we will talk about some practical ways that you and I can walk in innocence.

What do little children have that we often don't? How do they live their daily lives? They walk in innocence, freedom, and faith. Children get excited about the simplest of things. They enjoy the simple pleasures of life like you and I rarely do. Their days are spent in curiosity, exploration, and zeal. Recently our family sat down to watch some videos we shot when our kids were very young. One of those was of them opening presents on Christmas. Having ripped the paper off of a gift, our daughter Victoria was bubbling with joy and showing everyone the children's book she received. She declared, "Look what I got! Look what I got!" Everyone in the room was laughing; we thought it hilarious that anyone would get so excited over a book. When you choose to walk in simplicity and innocence before the Lord, you set yourself apart from those around you. Soon your life too will declare, "Look what I got!" Others will take notice, commenting that you seem so at peace, joyful, and carefree. People long for that freedom, joy, and innocence. There's your opportunity to tell them about the Jesus who gave it to you. Oh, if we would just return to living as free as a child.

Children approach each day with a sense of openness. There are no cares from the previous day dragged into the present. There is no agenda for the day, no "to do" lists. They don't wake up in the morning with a heavy burden on their heart. Perhaps the most telling characteristic of children is their ability to trust and believe. They trust their mom and dad to take care of them each day. It's not a conscious thought. They have grown up under the umbrella of love in their household. When something frightens them, they run to take refuge in that safe place—the loving arms of their parents. When the storm passes, they know it is safe to venture back out; they stay close to their shield of protection. All the burdens of life are carried and conquered by their parents. Provision for daily needs is taken for granted; it's a given. Food will be there on the table in the morning; worry does not exist.

What do children lack? What is missing from their perspective and their ability to navigate through life? They lack maturity, knowledge, a sense of responsibility, and the wisdom that comes from experience. That's why parents try to build character in their child that includes a sense of caring for others, a good work ethic, and a moral compass. *So we know that the call to become like a child is not a call to be foolish, selfish, or careless. That would violate maturity, wisdom, and responsibility. The call to become like a child is a call to return to the simplicity of innocence.*

When you really believe you are a child, and endeavor to live like one, you are empowered. Psalm 116:6 says, "The Lord protects the simple-hearted; when I was in great need, he saved me." What does it mean to be simple-hearted? It means that you are not burdened with the cares of this life. Here are some practical steps for you to become like a child—to experience the restoration of innocence in your life:

- *Don't drag your cares from the previous day into today.*
- *Learn to enjoy the simple pleasures of life.*
- *Don't ever wake up in the morning with a burden on your heart.*
- *Treat each day like it is a fresh start to life.*
- *Live like all your needs are going to be met by God, and you have no worries at all.*
- *Start to dance each day—allow your heart to be carefree. Dance like you have just discovered love for the very first time.*
- *Allow yourself a day of rest—maybe two—each week. Don't allow any agenda on these days. Be refreshed in your relationship with God on these days of rest.*
- *Allow your heart to be filled with hope on these special days— then carry that newly-found hope into the rest of your week.*

THE RESOLUTION OF FREEDOM

Freedom is a choice. When we are steadfast and determined in our pursuit of freedom, we don't give up until we have obtained it. We make a resolution that we will lay hold of it at all cost. The resolution we make as believers is this: If Jesus Christ shed his blood to purchase my freedom—I'm going to walk in that freedom—no matter what it takes. After all, this is our calling! "You, my brothers, were called to be free." (Gal. 5:13a) That's why the command from God is to stand firm. Galatians 5:1 tells us, "It is for freedom that Christ has set us free. Stand firm, then, and do not let yourselves be burdened again by a yoke of slavery." To become like a child, we must walk in freedom like young children do.

I have identified three characteristics of a child that we need to focus on to accomplish this resolution of freedom. They are: 1) The trust of a child; 2) The power of wholeness; 3) The freedom to dance. We can live in a freedom that is so sweet and real that it takes our breath away and refreshes our soul. So let's take a brief look at each of these three characteristics. Each of these will be relatively simple, as should be expected in order to "become like a child".

RESOLUTION #1—THE TRUST OF A CHILD

The old saying that trust is earned, while true, has a very real exception in the case of young children. A child is born into trust from the moment he leaves his mother's womb. Rather than being earned because of the actions of the parents, trust is something built-in to every child by God. Later in life that same trust can be further developed, strengthened, or lost. Even when children have been wounded by the actions of their parents, there is still the opportunity for trust to be re-entered. Of course, this is no easy endeavor. But children quickly make the choice to forget an offense—and so must we.

Trust is so hard to master in one's life. It takes incredible vulnerability. Yet it seems quite natural for a young child. In this case, it is more of a natural instinct than a learned behavior. With young children, there is no past performance to base trust upon. There is no failure on the part of the parent to warrant distrust either. To become like a child and enter into trust, you must become completely vulnerable with God. Following the simple steps below is not a "cure-all" formula. I don't know if I actually like that term because everything you lack—Jesus is. He's not a formula, but He sure is the cure for whatever we need. Let me just say that if you follow these steps and grow in trust, you will begin to experience the freedom that children walk in.

Keeping it simple:

- *Allow God into the areas of your life where trust has been damaged.*
- *Allow the Lord to heal those wounds.*
- *Grab your heavenly Father's hand, like a child would, and make a resolution that you will trust again.*
- *Start with trusting God again, then work your way (with His help) towards trusting others.*
- *Remember that children always run home to the security of their parents' love. The more intimate you get with God, the more you will give your heart away, trust, be vulnerable, and walk in love. Always run home to God.*

RESOLUTION #2—THE POWER OF WHOLENESS

Where do I begin with this one? I would like to start with a discussion about the broken condition that many find themselves in. Then wholeness could be viewed in contrast to a state of depravity in mankind. However, I am not going to do that. Instead, I will set my focus on the power that you and I can have when we learn how to "become like a child". Then wholeness can be understood in simple terms. That's the way it should be anyway. God doesn't make it complicated for us. Love, faith, and obedience—these form the foundation for understanding the kingdom of God.

We all desire to be made whole. We know that we have already been made righteous with the righteousness of Christ. "God made him who had no sin to be sin for us, so that in him we might become the righteousness of God." (2Cor. 5:21) We are not talking about some kind of wholeness that either exists outside of Jesus, or can be obtained separate from that which we already have as a child of God. If we have been made whole in Christ, then what are we talking about? The answer is more than just feelings.

The goal is not to simply feel whole. The goal is to live like Christ lived. That means we believe, act, and live like those who are whole. That is the power of wholeness. We walk in that power through the simplicity, innocence, and freedom of a child. The wholeness you experience will not only set you free, it will have a domino effect on those around you. Wholeness has a very strong, alluring effect. It draws people in from miles away. A person who walks in wholeness is content, settled in their faith, and at peace in their soul. They never wear you down or sap all the energy out of you. They are healed emotionally; they are looking to give to others. They are great encouragers. Everyone wants to be around a person who is whole. They refresh the presence of those that are blessed to spend time with them.

Keeping it simple:

- *The key to wholeness is what you believe.*
- *Start by believing God is so deeply in love with you that He is crazy about you.*
- *Believe you are beautiful in God's eyes—right now, just as you are.*
- *Believe that you are completely forgiven; that you are as fresh and clean as a newborn baby in God's eyes.*

- *Now forgive yourself; let yourself off the hook. Cast all of your cares onto Him.*
- *Spend the next several days and weeks just meditating on these truths. Breathe in God's wholeness.*
- *Make a list of people you know that desperately need to find and experience God's wholeness. Go share these truths with them. Stick with them until they experience the power of wholeness in their own life.*

RESOLUTION #3—THE FREEDOM TO DANCE

One of the greatest joys of our reward in heaven will be the freedom that we immediately will discover. The moment we leave this earthly shell, better known as our bodies, we will experience a freedom like no other. No more sickness or pain, every burden lifted from our shoulders. Fear and death will not be found. Imagine not being tired. There will be no shame; nothing to be embarrassed about. Our entire glorified being will erupt with pleasure. You and I, my friend, will break out into dancing. With every yoke broken, and no more cares of life to bear, we will sing and dance in liberty.

That is a wonderful thing to think about. I'm sure you are excited with anticipation of that moment, just as I am. Yet I didn't write this book to talk about the freedom we will experience in the future. We have that freedom in Christ today. I want to talk to all of those who long to experience that freedom in their lives right now. Is that you? Let's talk about how you can enjoy that freedom and dance like you have always dreamed of. In chapter nine, we will talk about how to discover the song that makes us dance before the Lord. But once again, let's prime the pump in anticipation of those future pleasures.

The freedom to dance always involves a willingness to be on the dance floor with no cares. You must not care who is watching. You must not care what they think. And you certainly must not care how you look. It's no wonder that children can run, skip, and dance with so much freedom. Their concerns are different than adults. But what if you could change that today? What if today was a day of transformation for you and me? What would it look like? Would it be embarrassing, or simply beautiful?

Have you ever done something out of the ordinary, like getting up at the early hours of the morning and spending time with Him, just to be in His presence? Our souls long for that kind of release. Why would you do that? Because your soul longs to spend another ten or fifteen minutes with Him! You can't sleep—not because of the worries and cares of this life—not because you need to "wrestle it out" with God. It's because you love Him! Your soul can't get enough of His sweet presence; your soul longs for the Lord more than your body desires sleep. *This is where you learn to dance with the Lord. It's not when you have come to the end of yourself—that's when you find salvation. It's when you come to the point that you have fallen head-over-heels in love with God. You are no longer mindful of yourself. It really wouldn't matter if anyone was watching at this point. You are loved, forgiven, and free. Dancing begins when there is no more hesitation between you and God.*

Go ahead—find yourself a place to be alone with Him. Fall at Jesus' feet and worship Him, or sit and stare into His wonderful eyes. Don't say a thing. Ah! That's hard, isn't it? We are not very good at that. Let's go a little further than that. Let Him talk to you; let God touch you. Let Him hold you. Let the Lord whisper into your ear the romantic words that only lovers can share with one another. Let Him be God. He is the pursuer; you are the object of His affection.

My friend, do not deny those desires you have to dance with Jesus, the Lover of your soul. Such desires are wholly God-given. The freedom to dance is only enjoyed by those who allow these desires to move them to action. But you cannot dance with someone you do not know. You can, but it is kind of awkward, isn't it? Exactly! You only feel comfortable dancing with someone you know—intimately. That's when you are able to skip and dance, much like a young girl does on the playground. For the child, the freedom to dance comes when no one is watching, or she is in the presence of those who love her the most. In the mind of a young child—that's nearly all of the time! That is the place you and I need to get to. That is a place of intimacy; it's a place of romance. Now you are on the verge of an intimate relationship with God. Proceed! Let the dance begin.

THE RESILIENCE OF FAITH

If you don't make it through the rest of this book, make this chapter the only one you remember. If you find yourself having a hard time relating to what I am writing on this subject—good for you. For everyone else, I believe God wrote this chapter with you in mind.

What does it mean to be resilient? According to Webster it means "an ability to recover from or adjust easily to change or misfortune." Children easily forget and bounce back from events that shake most adults. More than that, they are able to place their trust once again in an individual who has just failed or hurt them the day before. Simple childlike faith is resilient. This is the kind of faith that we need. How does a child deal with disappointment and failure? They overcome it by quickly forgetting and moving on. You and I must do the same.

Let it be known that God has not, and will not, fail you. It has never happened; it cannot happen. The Bible says, "The Scripture says, No man who believes in Him (who adheres to, relies on, and trusts in Him) will (ever) be put to shame or be disappointed." (Rom. 10:11 AMP) I love the way the Message Bible puts it:

> Scripture reassures us, 'No one who trusts God like this—heart and soul—will ever regret it.' It's exactly the same no matter what a person's religious background may be: the same God for all of us, acting the same

> incredibly generous way to everyone who calls out for
> help. Everyone who calls, 'Help, God!' gets help. (Rom.
> 10:11-13 MSG)

Any disappointment that you believe you have had with God
is based off of your perception of past experiences. Together with
your emotions, these past experiences led you to make erroneous
assumptions about God's character, and His plan for your life. Your
trust in God was tried. But you need to place that trust in Him
again, just like a child would. God is faithful; He cannot change.

Have you ever been disappointed with God? It's hard to even
say, isn't it? It seems wrong to even think such a thing, doesn't it?
Go ahead—you can admit it. God is not going to strike you down
for thinking such a thought. To disappoint is "to fail to fulfill the
expectation or hope of".[7] God is faithful, good, and perfect love;
it is impossible for Him to disappoint someone. Yet when we see
through the eyes of mere experience, rather than faith, it is often
possible that we feel this sense of disappointment. We didn't get
what we wanted. We didn't get what we felt we needed. But God
promised it in His Word. How can that be? We get frustrated,
confused, and yes, disappointed. I know I have experienced a lack
of fulfillment in regards to my expectations and hopes many times.
I don't let it dissuade me. I get right back up and grab onto the same
expectations, hopes, and dreams that I had before.

Have you ever suffered the dreaded "buyer's remorse" when
purchasing something? We all know the feeling. It hits the hardest
when your hope is at a heightened level. You did all your homework,
studied the latest copy of Consumer's Guide, and went out and
purchased that car. After two months of visits to the auto repair
shop, with your head in your hands and a hole in your wallet, you
find yourself drifting between indignation and acrimony. Good

---

[7] The New Merriam-Webster Dictionary(Springfield, Mass: Merriam-
Webster Publishers, 1989)

thing it was a car and not a house. There's nothing like the feeling of moving in and finding out all the things you overlooked or was never told about. I remember driving slowly through the neighborhood we now live in, several times, before we finally made an offer on our house. It wasn't until the day we moved in that I noticed a German shepherd in the front yard of my neighbor's house across the street. And of course this one barks every time someone passes by. Great!

Christians are good at telling a partial story to potential customers. One of the things I love about the Bible is the fact that the Holy Spirit just tells it as it is. There are so many stories of lives that are just messed up. Even the people we admire, our "Bible Heroes", had flawed lives. Look at King David. He had everything a man could want—power, wealth, and women. He decides that's not good enough, steals another man's wife, and then has that man murdered. He not only had what every man could want, he had much more. Power, wealth, and women are what the flesh of man craves. But he also had what the spirit in man needs—an intimate relationship with his Lord. And he still chose the sinful actions. The Bible tells the story as it is, so why can't we? The partial story we tell is somehow designed to not scare the customer away.

I know you don't regret the decision you made to follow Jesus. You are not suffering from "buyer's remorse", wishing you had never trusted your life in God's hands. But some of you are living in disappointment right now in your relationship with God. Many others have done so in the past. I know it's not easy to shake off our hurt, disappointment, and failures; it's not easy to be as carefree as a child. Yet that is the resilience of faith. The faith of a child never quits; it simply keeps on believing, day after day. You may think that you got your hopes up too high. That's not true; it's impossible to get your hopes too high when you put your hope in God. You may feel that you put all your trust and hope in God, and He didn't come through for you—**yet!**

Ah! Now that's the key. What does yet mean? It means you are still alive, there's still time, and it's not too late. You can start believing God again, trusting your heavenly Father to come through for you, putting all your hope in Him saving you out of whatever mess or heartbreaking situation your life is currently in. That's precisely what I do. I hold onto hope. I literally wake up in the morning saying to myself, "God is going to come through for you!"

Whenever I think about the resilience of faith I am reminded of a portion of scripture that is very dear to me. It gives me hope when I feel disappointed. It helps me to not want to quit. It fills me with expectation that I will soon experience the goodness of God in my own life. It's a story that Jesus told. Now I know why He told the story. He was thinking about me. Jesus was thinking about you. He knew we would struggle and need encouragement. The story is found in the gospel of Luke, chapter 18.

The parable begins by telling us why Jesus told it. "Then Jesus told his disciples a parable to show them that they should always pray and not give up." (Luke 18:1) In verse eight Jesus ties in faith to prayer. "However, when the Son of Man comes, will he find faith on the earth?" (Luke 18:8b) He is saying that when you pray, it should be done in faith. That means you are persuaded that what you are asking for is the will of God; you are confident that He has granted your request. That causes you to have hope, which means you are expecting something good from God. As you read the parable you see how Jesus is encouraging us. The story culminates in this statement by Jesus: "And will not God bring about justice for his chosen ones, who cry out to him day and night? Will he keep putting them off? I tell you, he will see that they get justice, and quickly." (Luke 18:7-8)

What is the message here? The resilience and persistence of faith pays off! Don't let disappointment overtake you. Don't let go of hope. The Lord will grant justice and mercy to His children who cry out to Him in faith. God rewards those who, with persistent faith, walk in the steps of a child.

CHAPTER 7

Now What Do I Do?

KEY #2—SIMPLIFY YOUR LIFE

It doesn't get much easier than what lies before us. If we only knew the simplicity of the path we tread upon—we would never venture far from it like some in search of a better way.

eah…right! I just heard everyone say that in response to this idea. It's not easy, yet it is the desire of all who live busy, hectic lives. That means the majority of us. *When God's people decide to move from the place of busyness to the position of simplicity, you will hear a collective sigh of relief echo through the chambers of the church, and you will be part of that plan of exodus.*

If the process of simplifying your life causes you to fall deeper in love with Jesus, and develop an intimacy with Him, you have clearly put God's kingdom first. However, if you make these changes only for the reason of creating balance, more time in your life, and less chaos, this chapter serves little purpose for you. I can help you change your lifestyles, but an intimacy with God will radically transform your entire life. Which do you want?

Paul wrote to the church in Corinth:

> For I am jealous for you with a godly jealousy; for I
> betrothed you to one husband, that to Christ I might
> present you as a pure virgin. But I am afraid, lest as
> the serpent deceived Eve by his craftiness, your minds
> should be led astray from *the simplicity and purity of*
> *devotion to Christ.* (2Cor. 11:2-3 NAS)

Every believer is in desperate need of applying this to their life. So what does it mean to simplify your life? What will it take to accomplish this? What do you need to do to return to "the simplicity and purity of devotion to Christ"?

To simplify your life is to make a deliberate choice for change. It involves surrender; it involves how you think, what you believe, and how you approach each day. You need to take the necessary actions that make a statement about your sincerity. I suggest when you put this book down you talk to God about your desire to change. Don't bring your day-timer schedule book or your watch into your time alone with God. *God is not impressed by those who have their act together, or those who have a busy schedule but manage it well. Do you want to know what gets His attention? "This is the one I esteem: he who is humble and contrite in spirit, and trembles at my word." (Isaiah 66:2b)*

Humble yourself before God. Boil your life down to where there's just you and Jesus. Life takes on a new meaning at this place. You find yourself not wanting to leave God's presence. The busy agenda fades into the background. **Life then becomes very simple, yet not because there is simply nothing to do. We simplify our life when nothing else matters in life but God, and Him alone!**

Start with repentance; confess to God the sins that He convicts your heart about. It's not a sin to be busy. But it is a sin to <u>allow</u> busyness, or anything else, to come between you and God. So maybe you need to repent of the sin of neglecting God. Maybe you have not put His kingdom first. Perhaps your heart is devoted to other things, and busyness becomes an excuse that conceals the place where your passions and desires really abide.

The next step involves the care of your soul—your mind, will, and emotions. This is something both you and your family need to do, as individuals and collectively. *It involves having a mindset of simplicity and an attitude of peace, no matter how frenzied your life is. Be determined to simplify your life at all cost. Dedicate yourself, your family, and your schedule to the Lord before you begin to make changes. In your heart develop an attitude of simplicity. Devote yourself to finding God in intimacy as an end result.* Start here; don't start with laying out your daily schedule of events and eliminating the ones you don't need to do. Remember that the goal is intimacy, not self-help. A motivational speaker can help you bring order to your busy life. But only God, your *Creator*, can bring about lasting change by *creating* order and peace inside your restless soul.

I remember a Christian friend stopping over at our house for a visit several years ago. She didn't stay long, but before she left she turned to my wife and I and remarked, "It's so peaceful at your house. It's not that way at our house; things are so hectic." This woman sensed something in the spirit; something was different. She was attracted to the peaceful atmosphere in our home. To us it was just another day. We had plenty to keep us busy with young children running around the house. But we chose an attitude of peace. We chose to live a very simple lifestyle.

At our house we have a plaque in the kitchen in the shape of a hen that reads, "I put all my eggs into one basket—and gave the basket to God!" You need to release everything to God; give Him the basket. There is time for everything when God is in control of your time. Give Him your plans for the future, your busy schedule for the day, and your restless heart. Set your heart on Him first, trusting Him to take care of you. His peace will guard your heart and mind, and you will find a new strength to approach life's battles on a daily basis. He knows you have a lot to get done today; He knows you have a lot on your mind. But do you really trust Him to take care of those things for you?

This demands great vulnerability on your part. Will my work get done if I put God first and spend time today praying and seeking Him? The solution is not a self-made orderly life, brought about by discipline. It's not about working smarter, harder, or doing less. It's all about relationship. You start with faith, trust, and commitment.

> Trust in the Lord and do good; dwell in the land and enjoy safe pasture. Delight yourself in the Lord and he will give you the desires of your heart. Commit your way to the Lord; trust in him and he will do this: He will make your righteousness shine like the dawn, the justice of your cause like the noonday sun. (Psalm 37:3-6)

Finally, once you have begun this process of simplifying your life, you continue to walk in it by faith. No matter how busy your life becomes, you never take that basket back from God's hands. When an individual views his life in the light of his circumstances, busyness becomes an excuse. When a believer views his life in the light of Christ, those circumstances take on a new meaning. Then everything in life becomes an opportunity for surrender, rather than a burden.

KEY #3—APPROACH GOD WITH CONFIDENCE

The tragedy of not looking into the face of God with confidence is much too great a thing to bear. Confidence before God is not derived from man's greatness. It doesn't necessarily rise to the surface in times of man's overwhelming sense of need. We often see God's own people lacking such confidence. How can this be? I believe this lack of confidence begins at a young age for most of us, and continues through our adult years. Often going unnoticed, it affects every area of our life. Fear attacks us when we most need a shot of boldness to accomplish a task, or approach someone in relationship, and confidence simply slips away and hopes for yet another day.

The confidence to approach God is not found at the end of the journey, it is formed throughout. You must not allow your experiences to affect your approach to the altar of God. You must be sure of yourself in your approach. Much greater than mere self assurance, an unwavering confidence in the character of God will set your heart and mind at ease as you approach Him. It needs to be the kind of confidence that has deep roots. This is a process; it takes time. An oak tree doesn't grow up overnight. But when it does, it is unmovable. There is no panic in a time of drought; the roots are deep enough to handle any storm or famine.

Sometimes a child desires to play games with his dad. At other times, just simply spending time together is enough. During times such as these, the child is content to be in the same room as his father, no matter what he is doing. The child finds comfort in the knowledge that his father is near. When the child feels comfortable with his dad, he doesn't hesitate to approach him and ask him for something—anything he needs. But there are so many things that affect the child's approach, so there needs to be a constant reassuring from the parents to the child of the accessibility and freedom he has.

Such was the case with our son Josiah when he was younger. When he wanted to watch a football or basketball game on television, which he would do all day if we allowed him to, he would ask my wife for permission. Why didn't he ask me? It wasn't because he knew I would say no, but because he was <u>afraid</u> I would say no. I usually gave him permission to watch TV. So why was he still apprehensive to ask? Because past experience had taught him that I had said no, and perhaps had been harsh in doing so. Thus the perfect remedy is constant encouragement from me that I love him. My son has the freedom to ask me anything, and I'm not going to get angry with him for asking.

It takes a long time, however, for change to occur in one's approach. I want Josiah to come to me first. He knows I have shown him kindness in the past. He knows I have instructed him over and over again that he has an open door to my heart. Yet still he would hesitate. It took a great deal of time for him to feel comfortable and build trust in me as his dad, especially after a few negative experiences. I'm not the perfect parent, so I continue to work on this area in my life.

Do you see the correlation here to our relationship with God? Trust in our heavenly Father is built up over a long period of time, yet not because of failure on God's part. He is the perfect Father, even when we think He is not (many would never admit to having such a thought). We develop an approach to God based on certain criteria (i.e. Is God trustworthy? Will God come through for me? Is God harsh with His children?) So our confidence in Him may be shaky at best if we falsely perceive those criteria have not been adequately met.

Just look at our prayer life. Why are you and I so fidgety in His presence? We are as squirmy as a young child trying to sit still during a lengthy Sunday morning worship service. What's worse is the reality that you and I are more comfortable in a hundred other situations outside of time alone with God. One would hope that this all changes the longer we follow God. Does it? There should be a dramatic change, yet to a certain degree, there will always be a smidgen of restlessness in the presence of the Lord this side of heaven. *As we grow in intimacy and confidence our hearts become settled; the restlessness subsides.*

If you feel uncomfortable in your approach to God—just tell Him. Talk to Him about it; believe God's Word to change you. "In him (Christ) and through faith in him we may approach God with freedom and confidence." (Eph. 3:12) When we approach God in this way it pleases Him, because to do so takes a demonstration of faith. In fact, when we move toward God with confidence, we are saying that we trust Him. And when God knows that we are walking in confidence before Him, he responds to us: "So do not throw away your confidence; **it will be richly rewarded**." (Heb. 10:35)

Confidence is always based upon the character of the one you are placing your confidence in. Start by relaxing in God's presence when you pray. Imagine that God has just invited you to spend time with Him, as if you are the only one on the face of the earth, and the only thing on His heart right now is to spend time with you. That's a healthy recipe right there. You will soon find yourself growing in confidence.

KEY #4—DISCOVER YOUR BEAUTY TO GOD

In chapter eleven we will discuss this subject at a greater length, especially as it pertains to walking in beauty before God. But before we can do that, we need to first discover what this is. It's not that we don't understand beauty. In a strange way, we understand it all too well. It has an alluring nature to it. We are drawn like a magnet to the very presence of beauty whenever we come in contact with its various forms. Beauty has an element of great power. Men and women have taken this element and forged it into a tool. Using it as a tool, we have abused its inherent power. The abuse occurs through manipulation, flaunting, judging, comparing, and esteeming too highly the value of outward beauty. These forms of abuse keep us from walking in true beauty.

Once you discover your beauty to God, you will experience a freedom like you have never experienced before. But until you reach that point in your walk with Christ, you remain locked in a room. In that room, you are all alone—just you and a mirror. You gaze into the mirror looking at the same sight you have beheld for years. It disappoints you once again. *You won't find your beauty by looking in the mirror. You will find it in His presence—or you won't find it at all.* The glass slipper is not Cinderella's; it belongs to you. The great Initiator has spared no expense pursuing you. Will you tell the Holy Spirit you have no dress fit for the ball?

Your beauty will not fail you at midnight. You may feel like a failure. Perhaps you once walked away. But now God refers to you as the bride of Christ. Can you see all of creation pause as you dance with the Lord? The sun and moon stand at attention as the doors of the church swing open; the beauty created for Jesus enters in. Are you embarrassed? Just come. Come as you are. Stay for the dance. You are the object of His desire—the center of attention. Every eye is always fixed on the bride.

What is this beauty that you possess? It has power far beyond your understanding. Your beauty is this: you are created in the image of God; you bear His likeness; you are a co-heir to God's kingdom with Christ. You are the brother or sister of Jesus! You wear God's beauty as a garment. When God looks at you, He is looking into the face of Jesus, because you are in Christ. *The beauty you possess is alluring to your God; it is a sweet fragrance to Him.* We have great reason to believe that there is other life in the universe. The book of Revelation talks about some of the heavenly creatures we will see some day soon. But no one is as beautiful as you. God may have created millions of other creatures for all we know—we don't know, actually—but one thing is sure—only you were created in His image. And only you did He send His Son to die for.

You are the beauty Jesus desires to be with. Will you believe and enter into intimacy? *This truth will literally blow you away when you do. You need to personalize it. I can point to this as one of the major turning points in my walk with God. When I discovered my beauty in God's eyes, I was set free.* The more I meditated on it, and the deeper I believed it, the more I could relate to God as my lover. Often in prayer I'll say to God, "You just can't get enough of me. I know it; it's true." God is crazy about you! He's whipped over His bride! Would you expect anything less from the God who is love? Now start believing it.

This cannot be accomplished through education. You can't take a class and usher yourself in. It is relatively easy to get someone to accept that they are a sinner and need God. It is extremely difficult to get them to believe they are beautiful in God's eyes. That's why many never experience intimacy. They know God as their savior to a great degree, but they seldom enter into the lover relationship with Him. They can't see themselves as God's beauty—the one He is madly in love with.

CHAPTER 8

Time to Enjoy

KEY #5—DELIGHT YOURSELF IN THE LORD

There's something about God that makes us want to shout, sing, laugh, dance, be still, and rest our heads on His lap as we gaze into His beautiful eyes—all at the same time. There's something about God that leaves us speechless—we simply don't know what to say. We don't know what to do. To delight in Him—to worship Him—that's all we can. That's all we need to. There's something about God—our souls just can't get enough.

What a topic to try to wrap your arms around. To delight oneself in God—what a wonderful thought! My mind can't embrace what to do once I have my arms around Him. He's too much to hold, too much to handle, and too beautiful to behold. The language of mankind is at a loss for words. Is it possible to experience God at such a deep level that our lives are changed forever? It all starts here.

Delight yourself in the Lord. That sounds nice, doesn't it? It sounds appealing; the phrase offers freedom. But Christianity is more than just a nice story. We walk in power when we delight in the Lord because we are obeying God's Word. "Delight yourself in the Lord and he will give you the desires of your heart." (Psalm 37:4) People quote this verse and get pretty excited. It is exciting to think of God granting us the desires of our heart. Yet it is more exciting to ponder the first half of the verse.

I'm sure you treasure the days in your life which are most memorable, as I do. That's true for any special day we experience, but I want to talk specifically about spiritual "special" days. Those are days that transform your life. We remember them as life-changing, dramatic experiences. They are not merely experiences, but moments in our lives when God moves in such a real and intimate way, touching every fiber of our being.

Think back to some of those days in your own life. It may have been a day of provision, where something you had been seeking God for suddenly showed up in your life. It may have been a day of encouragement, where God sent a friend to lift you up and refresh you when you were at the end of your rope in need. These days take on various forms. Often it is a retreat or seminar experience, a sermon, or simply a personal time in prayer at your house. If you are a believer, you have certainly had at least one such experience—the day you gave your life to Christ. The longer you follow Jesus, stay connected, and walk in obedience to Him, the more of these days you will have.

When you delight yourself in the Lord, you set yourself up to experience this kind of day on a regular, frequent basis. If that is not enough to get you interested in delighting yourself in the Lord, nothing else will. The more you experience God, the more you are going to want to experience God. Especially as you discover His will for your life. That will excite you. The result of that excitement is you choosing to delight in God spontaneously. It will become so unplanned and natural that you find yourself doing it all day long.

What if we approached God radically different than we do today? What if we approached Him in a new way? I recommend that we do just that. And that "new" way is the way of delight.

Psalm 37 makes it clear that we are to make the Lord the object of our delight. We cannot delight, unless we have been delighted in, and know it at the core of our being. "We love because he first loved us." (1John 4:19) All three thoughts are connected, perfectly woven

84

together by the Lord. God delights in us—we delight in Him—He gives to us the desires of our heart. It is a spiritual law, ordained by God. He took pleasure in establishing it that way. God takes great joy in giving His children the desires of their heart. Yet there is a definite order of events that needs to take place for this to happen. This order is God's way of keeping us from covetousness.

What does this Christian who delights in the Lord look like? It's the child of God who believes that his daddy is good. It's the child of God who runs into his father's presence. It's the child of God who does not look at prayer as a burden, but as a joy. This child skips into God's presence. He is not afraid of knocking something over in the room, and getting yelled at. He doesn't feel like an interruption or inconvenience to God. He is comfortable in his father's presence. This child of God knows how to delight in the Lord. It comes natural for him. He has been doing it for years. The child waits in the throne room of the Lord, because Father God has promised to take him fishing today. He enjoys spending time with his dad. His daddy has always been good to him; his father has always kept His promise to him; he trusts in his father's love.

Did you enjoy that description? I could be describing you, if you will just start delighting in the Lord today. For many believers, spending time with God has become as rigid and ritualistic as brushing and flossing their teeth. It's done because we have to; it's expected of us. It's done with very little enthusiasm or urgency, except for those times in our lives where a crisis is staring us in the face. We apply no value to spending an hour or two with God, because we really don't believe it will make a difference in our lives. We think "what's the use?"

The value we place on spending time with God is low, because somewhere inside of us, we don't think it's worth it. Therefore we make a daily declaration of the things we value by the way our time is spent. We reap what we have sown. We expect little; we have little. God will give us grace to change, but we have a part in this story, a part that determines the outcome.

Oh, you're saved. You know the Lord Jesus personally. But you could have had so much more! You could have known Him intimately. You could have had more of His kingdom (which He delights in giving to His children). You had not because you asked not. (James 4:2) Like the Israelites in the wilderness, you didn't really believe. So you ended up living your life wandering in the desert, even while your soul desired so much more of God.

*I have never seen the 1986 movie <u>Children of a Lesser God</u>. I have no idea what it is actually about. But if there is any indictment against the Church today, it is this—**we have become Children of a Lesser God**. It's not because God is weak. It's not because His Word doesn't work. It's not because He doesn't move today like He used to. It's because of the way we have chosen to live. We have made His Word of no effect in our lives.*

If this describes your life today, then close this book right now, and call upon the name of the Lord. Cry out to God. Knock and the door will be opened; seek and you will find; ask and it shall be given to you. Just say, "Lord, I don't want my life to end this way. I want more of you. I want all of you. I want to know you intimately. Help me to desire you. Teach me how to delight in you."

To "delight yourself in God" is the most wonderful and rewarding thing that you could ever do with the rest of your life down here on earth. This way of life is not designed for heaven only. It's for you—right here, right now. Ask God to help you delight in Him. *Every snowflake is unique in its design. Your way of interacting with and delighting in God will look different than mine. Yet it will be just as exciting, just as wonderful, and just as fulfilling.*

To delight in someone is to take great pleasure in them. You become filled with joy at the very sight of them. When we have experienced God's delight in us we obtain a sense of belonging. We are secure in His delight and respond in kind. "He brought me out into a spacious place; he rescued me because he delighted in me." (Psalm 18:19) David knew that the Lord delighted in him. "Keep me as the apple of your eye", he said to the Lord. (Psalm 17:8) For many, the hardest part is convincing themselves that God really does delight in them. Once they really believe it, then they have the confidence to draw near to God, and begin delighting in Him.

When you delight in God, you give Him every passion, desire, and dream you have. It's not hard to identify competing delights in your life. If you think about it right now with any level of honesty, you can come up with a short list. Those areas of life where your passion and time is invested will continue to have a strong pull on you. Decide today that you will allow nothing to compete with God for first place in your heart. Ask God to help you transfer that desire to Him, and His kingdom.

Please note—if your greatest love and passion is towards your children, choosing to delight in God does not mean you no longer delight in them. It means that now you are making a conscious effort, by the grace of God, to put the things of God and His kingdom first in your life. As you delight in God, your children will see a living example of where they are to place their delight. They will observe Mom and Dad giving all their joy, passions, time, and energy to seeking, serving, and loving God. In fact, you couldn't do anything greater for your children than to choose to delight in the Lord, often and daily. Your children will hear you singing to God, and they'll know what you are thinking about. They will see you on your knees and spending a lot of time in the Word, and they will know who is number one with Mom and Dad—and it's not them!

Okay, let's be practical. How do we do this? How does one delight himself in God? Let me tell you one of the practical ways I used to delight myself in the Lord. I used to call it "taking God golfing". If you ever saw me golf, you would sure hope I would take God with me, just to help me play better. But that's a different story. Anyway, it was an agreement or understanding that God and I had with each other. It was typically rather spontaneous. It was similar to a man and woman saying to each other, "Hey, let's do something tonight. Yeah, let's go out on a date." I would usually wait for a laid-back Sunday afternoon in the summer when the weather was pretty much perfect. Then I would say to God, "Hey, let's go golfing today, just you and I." God would always say yes. So off on our date we would go.

It was amazing how well I would play on these special golf outings with God. We had an agreement. I was to golf alone with God, and I was not to keep track of the score. If I got to the clubhouse and they tried to pair me up with one or two others, I simply declined; I insisted on golfing alone. I didn't take a scorecard with me. If you know anything about golf, it can be a very frustrating game, and it requires a great deal of concentration to play. On these days when I went golfing with God, He gave me the grace to relax, focus on Him, and not even think about the golf part. That's incredible in itself because every golf experience for me always has a sure measure of frustration. I remember one time I was shooting a very low score, better than I have ever golfed in my life. Even when you don't keep track of the score in golf, you know when you are having a good game. I was shooting par—birdie—then par—yet another par. Wait a minute. "Hey, Lord", I said. "I've never played this good in my life...I might shoot a..." Then God got my attention. A quiet voice inside my heart was God speaking to me. "Scott, you are here to spend time with me, remember?" With laughter I said, "Ok, Lord. I'm sorry; let's get back to just you and I hanging out again."

As far as I was concerned, it was like no one else was on the course on those days—just me and God! I treasure those memories. It was so intimate, so sweet. I spent the whole time singing to God. I would praise Him, and talk intimately with Him. Very little time was spent in intercession for others or praying about my needs. There's always time for that, my friend. But when you delight yourself in the Lord—it's time to dance! I would sing when I was hitting the ball, and sing while I was walking to my next shot. I sang as loud as I wanted to; I didn't care who heard me. You can't care about that if you choose to delight in God. All you need to care about is the eyes of the One who beholds you.

Now you go and find a way to delight yourself in the Lord. Make it unique; make it special. It will be special in the eyes of the Lord when you do. Perhaps some of you will get a cup of your favorite coffee, snuggle up with a blanket in your favorite chair, and read a great book. Bring the Lord with you. Snuggle up with Him; delight in Him. This leads exceptionally well into our next chapter on dancing with God.

CHAPTER 9

Dance Often with God

I have forgotten how to dance. I'm at the party, but I just can't seem to "get into it". I enjoy the people who are there...well, most of them at least. But right now I feel content to just sit back and watch. Come to think of it, as I look around the large gathering room, I'm not the only one. The music is still playing. There is an invitation to dance, but the dance floor is rather unoccupied at this moment. I don't know where I belong—on the sideline watching—or out on that lonely floor.

It's been such a long time. I feel uncomfortable about the thought of going out there. Maybe if I lead the way, others will follow. Perhaps today will be different. This could be the day my whole life changes. But what if I am the only one out on the floor? I find myself grasping for reasons to stay where I am. The more I hesitate, the harder it is to make my move. Let's just pretend everything is ok. Christians are good at that, right? I'm not a child anymore, so why act like one? Many years ago I would have been out there dancing, leading the way. But now my zeal is gone. Yet I'm content with who I am...until I realize who I could be. Let's not dance tonight; I don't want to think about it anymore.

*H*ave you ever felt like that? Even at some of our best moments—in the midst of dancing—we can be dying inside, and no one knows. We all have a song that we dance to. Even those who never physically dance have one. To dance here refers to that which motivates us, and that which brings delight to our souls as well. There is a button inside each of us that, when pushed, becomes the force which causes us to move. This button lights a fire in us. Sometimes we sing, at other times we dance.

If it is not a physical button that we can see, just what is it inside of us that ignites us to such passion? Some of you are old enough to remember the hit TV show Name That Tune. On the show, contestants would be given a clue about the name of a song. If one of them believed they knew the answer, they would say, "I can name that song in 'x' amount of notes." The contestant who was sure they could name the song in the least amount of notes would get a shot at it. His competitor would say, "Name that tune." So they would play one or two notes, and the contestant would have to guess. That's very difficult to do with any song of course. It's incredible how accurate they were at naming the tune.

I believe God has tailor-made a song to uniquely fit each one of us. God is an intimate God. He will lead you in ways that are very personal, that only you can relate to. We need to learn the ways of God, how to recognize His voice, and how He uniquely talks to each of us.

Do you know what song it is that makes you dance? God does. The intimate God of this universe is not far away, uninvolved and unaware. He knows what you prefer. He designed you that way. The Lord knows if you dance to the beat of summer, winter, spring, or fall. He is able to name that tune *in your life. Are you?*

Surely you have been at a wedding reception where the band is playing and a couple next to you says to each other, "C'mon honey— let's dance, they are playing our tune." What does that mean? Well, it means something to them that you don't know about. It's the song that they dance to. They don't need to listen to half the song to figure it out. They are quite familiar with the tune. The song brings back memories, stirs up their emotions, and causes passion to rise in their souls. **So it is in our walk with God. He has been weaving many themes into the story of our lives. These themes form the songs that cause us to dance with God.**

The ability to "name that tune" has to do with being able to recognize God's voice in your life. We need to be led by the Holy Spirit and learn how to hear God speaking to us. Jesus said,

> The man who enters by the gate is the shepherd of his sheep. The watchman opens the gate for him, and the sheep listen to his voice. He calls his own sheep by name and leads them out. When he has brought out all his own, he goes on ahead of them, and his sheep follow him because they know his voice. But they will never follow a stranger; in fact, they will run away from him because they do not recognize a stranger's voice. (John 10:2-5)

That's you and I. He made it clear that we <u>can</u> hear His voice, and <u>will indeed</u> hear it. The very terminology of "hearing God's voice", of course, conjures up a wide variety of thoughts in our minds. We actually make it much harder than it needs to be. Christians trip all over themselves, and God, trying to figure out what the Lord is saying to them. We don't want to stray from the topic of intimacy, but let me just say that one of the keys in hearing from God is obedience. God reveals Himself to those that obey Him. Jesus said,

> The person who has my commands and keeps them is the one who really loves Me; and whoever really loves Me will be loved by My Father, and I too will love him and will show (reveal, manifest) Myself to him. I will let Myself be clearly seen by him and make Myself real to him. (John 14:21 Amplified Bible)

To live a life of intimacy with God you need to hear God's voice—how He speaks to <u>you</u>. Then you will learn His ways. It is then that you will be able to "name that tune" to the song God sings over you. You will learn to dance with God. You will know and experience intimacy.

This song that causes you to dance—perfectly defines who you are. It is a beautiful, flawless melody, handcrafted by your Creator, written just for you. What does it mean? It means that there is a way that God moves in your life that is unique to you, and no one else. He designed you to dance at the moment you hear the first note.

Don't go looking for an actual song. This is not a song you would listen to on your radio or mp3 player. I'm not talking about merely some signal God gives that you hear with your ear, or a song that is assigned by Him to get you out on the dance floor, jumping for joy. This is the song of your life, the music of your soul.

Remember the account of Elijah on Mount Horeb, the mountain of God? After spending the night in a cave, the Lord spoke to him.

> The Lord said, 'Go out and stand on the mountain in the presence of the Lord, for the Lord is about to pass by.' Then a great and powerful wind tore the mountains apart and shattered the rocks before the Lord, but the Lord was not in the wind. After the wind there was an earthquake, but the Lord was not in the earthquake. After the earthquake came a fire, but the Lord was not in the fire. And after the fire came a gentle whisper. When Elijah heard it, he pulled his cloak over his face and went out and stood at the mouth of the cave. Then a voice said to him, 'What are you doing here, Elijah?' (1Kings 19:11-13)

Elijah knew God's voice; he knew God's ways. He knew which "tune" was being played that day. The Lord was not in the wind, earthquake, or fire. But the gentle whisper—that was God! How did Elijah know this? He had spent years sitting at God's feet, waiting on Him, listening for His voice. God's voice was a familiar song to Elijah. God's ways were a melody that played repeatedly in Elijah's mind.

Have you ever been somewhere and your mind starts picking up a beat? The words and melody to a song begin to play in your head before your ears actually hear the first sound. You are some distance away; you can't even faintly hear the slightest sound at all—or so you think. Because as you get closer to the room or area where music is being played, you find that it is the exact song that was being played in your mind. It seemed like it was impossible for you to have heard any notes to the song from that distance—yet you had that song on your mind already. That has happened to me numerous times. If the mind is that tuned in to a song, how much more is the spirit inside a man able to hear the song of God's voice? Amazing!

Songs have the ability to move us emotionally. But the song that God causes us to dance to transforms us—spiritually. Jesus said, "The Spirit gives life; the flesh counts for nothing. The words I have spoken to you are spirit and they are life." (John 6:63)

Psalm 119:54 states, "Your decrees are the theme of my song wherever I lodge." The psalmist had a personal song that he sang to God. Does God have a personal song that He sings to us, that He sings to no other? Think about it. You were created in God's image, unique in design. You were fearfully and wonderfully made and designed by God. (Psalm 139:14) Your life can reveal and give glory to God like no other life can. What is the song you sing to God? What is the song God sings as He delights in you?

Sometimes you will have profound experiences where you clearly hear God's voice. *Those memories of experiencing God in your life will be some of your favorite songs. They will form the "music" God has played in your life. When you think about it, you dance intimately with God.* You recognize it right away when you experience it again and again in your life. Like Elijah, you discern it, and are able to say, "That's God". Your spirit hears His voice and your mind says, "Yeah, that's God—that's how He always speaks to me and moves in my life." It becomes a theme in your life, a recurring theme.

God has often led me in very personal, intimate ways. So this theme of intimacy is incredibly woven into who I am. When He speaks to me, it's often along the lines of reminding me of the intimate covenant of love we have made to each other. And when I hear His voice, I dance. Let me give you an example of this.

HEARING HIS VOICE

It was just another day at work, or so I thought. I worked at a large retail store during my years in college. I sat down in the employee lunchroom to take a break midway through my shift. Sitting across the table from me was a young man I knew from high school. He was quite the character, often joking around, yet enjoyable to talk with. We talked about several different topics, nothing too weighty or meaningful. Suddenly and out of nowhere, he leans across the table, looks me in the eyes, and says, "Scott, God loves you!" He did this with a smirk on his face. I knew this man well enough to know he was just goofing off. So I thought, "Alright, I'll go with it. This gives me an opportunity to talk with him about Jesus perhaps." So I looked at him with a serious look on my face and said, "I know that, Rob. And you know what? God loves you too."

Well, he quickly changed the topic of discussion, and soon his break was over. He got up and returned to the sales floor, and I stayed and finished my break. Looking down at my watch, I realized my break was over, and I started heading out of the lunchroom. As I walked toward the exit door I was thinking about my conversation with Rob. Silently I prayed to the Lord. "Lord, thank you for using me in such a small way to tell someone about your love. I know you had me here just at the right time to talk with Rob."

That's when I was taken by surprise. Something happened that I will remember for the rest of my life. It felt like God had physically entered the room. His presence came all over me in a very pronounced, persuasive way. The hair on the back of my neck was standing up; I could feel His presence, like a thick blanket draped over me. I knew He was about to speak to me. In my spirit I heard His voice. It was not audible, but it may as well have been. It was no less real than if you were standing right in front of my face and spoke out loud to me. The words were crystal clear; His gentle voice penetrated my heart. God said, "Scott, you've got it wrong. I didn't send you to speak to Rob. I put Rob there to speak to you—to tell you that I love you! I will use anyone—even someone who does not know me—to tell you again and again that I love you."

Those words stopped me in my tracks. I could barely keep my composure. I turned the corner by the lunchroom and glanced at the door to the stockroom, wondering if I could make it to the door before completely losing it and weeping. I hurried to the door, opened it, and quickly ran to an aisle to shield myself from any onlookers, as I began to weep. I couldn't control myself. Overcome with emotion, I intensely wept with joy. It took me several minutes to settle down and regain my composure so that I could go back out to the sales floor.

That's how God has spoken to me over the years. It's always in a way that is so personal and intimate. The same theme arises in each encounter. I have made a covenant with God, and He with me. And He takes it very seriously. So much so that He seems to go out of His way to remind me of that covenant of love. That's the theme of my song, and God knows it well. It's the song that I dance to.

Ask God what song it is that He sings over your life. He will be faithful to show you. Like Paul said to the church in Philippi, "being confident of this, that he who began a good work in you will carry it on to completion until the day of Christ Jesus." (Phil. 1:6) It will take time to learn to hear God's voice in your life. But as you do, you will start dancing. In anticipation, your heart will leap with joy and recognize when God is about to speak and move in your life. This will become a theme that God will weave into your life, a special song that only you and God dance to. And the more you dance with God, the more intimate with Him you will become. **You have to believe that He has created you as a masterpiece. And it is His desire that all of His children become master musicians, skilled in the art of dance.**

CHAPTER 10

7 Reasons Why God's
Children Fail Intimacy

The delight of man is too high a price for many to pay. To win one's delight, the unthinkable must be accomplished. To give your delight, you must render your soul. That is reserved for a select few in our lives. All preservation of self is therefore extinguished at the apex of the thought. Many never leave the realm of self-service. There is no room in the inner circle of the heart for some. Yet we find four basic areas that mankind will allow his delight to be given toward: things, children, a lover, and God.

There are seven reasons why intimacy is seldom entered into. #1: It's hard! #2: It costs too much. #3: We are not desperate. #4: There's no room in our lives for it. #5: We don't think it's something we need. #6: We simply don't care! #7: Fear.

You will notice one thing missing from our list. I didn't feel a lack of knowledge was an appropriate reason. Like I said in chapter three, you have intimate knowledge of many things in life. You are the one who makes the choice about the things in life you will get to know and understand. Knowing God intimately is within your reach. It's easy for someone to say, "I don't know how to. I've never been taught how to have intimacy with God. And I'm just not sure what it is, or what it looks like." The reason why I don't accept this as a legitimate stumbling block is simple. **Intimacy with God is not a learned virtue. It is an obtained relationship. I can teach you how to dance. But I can't teach you how to dance with God.**

In defense of knowledge, however, there are some truths to be taught, and some wisdom to be learned. That's why I wrote this book. Yes, it is true—we don't know what intimacy looks like. We not only can't put our finger on it, we can't put any feet on the thought either, so it just kind of floats out there somewhere. We haven't been taught much about it. We have not seen it modeled enough. To our benefit the church has countless books on prayer, faith, and the Second Coming of Christ. Yet with our emphasis on sinners getting saved, once again—rightly so—we have not gotten far enough beyond the important, elementary truths of what to do after we become saved. There is an unspoken expectation of something happening within our souls that, alas, seldom does. We are not quite sure what that is. Well, maybe we know now. Sure we do. Our souls yearn for something more—intimacy.

By now the picture should be getting clearer. You have just read nine chapters on what intimacy looks like, and how to obtain it. You should be able to see, feel, and taste the pathway that will lead you to the intimacy you desire. Take courage, this life of intimacy is available to you. Let's take a closer look at each one of the seven roadblocks. Let me warn you first—it won't be an easy pill to swallow. God doesn't want you to be discouraged or depressed—ever! God wills it in you, and then He accomplishes the work in your life. (Phil. 2:13) It is His work. But there are some obstacles that stand in your way. Are you ready? Here we go. Here are the mountains that need to be moved.

REASON #1—IT'S HARD!

"There is a tide in the affairs of men, which taken at the flood, leads on to fortune. Omitted, all the voyage of their life is bound in shallows and miseries." ~Shakespeare

"In battle there is a crisis in every fight. There is a period of ten to fifteen minutes on which the issue of the battle depends. To gain this is victory; to lose it is defeat." ~Napoleon

The Greeks had a statue called opportunity. It depicted a man running on tip-toe with winged feet. On the front it had long, flowing hair. On the back, it was bald. You could grab it coming at you; you couldn't get it once you passed by.

All relationships are hard. Why should a relationship with God be any different? As long as on one end of the equation you have sinful man, you will find every relationship you enter into difficult, including one that involves intimacy with God. It's hard at times to pray, let's admit it. Perseverance is not fun. Right now as I write this sentence, I don't want to. I don't want to persevere through the finishing of this book. It's a "long haul". That's what a commitment to intimacy is—a long and arduous road.

That's the hard part—that one word—commitment! Have you ever quit a math problem exercise because it was too hard? We all have. No big deal. Just turn to the back of the book and find out what the answer is. Why put yourself through all of that torment when someone else has already done the hard work for you? It's hard work to seek God each day. Let's leave it up to our pastor to seek God for us. We can just go to church and let him tell us what God is like. *That's what some of us are doing in our walk with God.* Sounds good enough, right? No—wrong answer. We can't delegate the work to someone else. In this case, delegating the work would mean missing out on the benefits of the relationship.

I had a season in my life when I prayed for two hours every day. I decided in my heart that I wanted to do this, and firmly committed to carrying it out. My mind was prepared, and I had a list of people and prayer requests to lift up to my heavenly Father. I knew that combined with a period of praise and worship, I could persevere for two hours. This was entirely separate from my time of Bible study. I didn't crack open the Bible until the two hours was up. It wasn't easy to maintain this commitment. But I sure enjoyed the benefits of the relationship during this time. Desire was there, but I soon realized that I couldn't continue at a rate of two hours per day. Besides, I would rather pray five minutes with all my heart and soul, than try to accomplish some man-made goal while thinking I'm being more spiritual by praying for a long period of time. I've come a long way since then in my maturity. Yet I'm honest enough to admit—it's hard! But—oh, boy—it is fulfilling! It's worth every ounce of hardship, blood, sweat, and tears it takes to get there.

REASON #2—IT COSTS TOO MUCH

Intimacy is worship. Worship is costly. King David's actions spoke of what true worship meant to him. You may recall the story of when David counted the fighting men in Israel and Judah. The Lord judged David's actions by sending a plague on Israel. David's response was repentance, followed by worship.

> *On that day Gad (a prophet) went to David and said to him, 'Go up and build an altar to the Lord on the threshing floor of Araunah the Jebusite.' So David went up, as the Lord had commanded through Gad. When Araunah looked and saw the king and his men coming toward him, he went out and bowed down before the king with his face to the ground. Araunah said, 'Why has my lord the king come to his servant?' 'To buy your threshing floor,' David answered, 'so I can build an altar to the Lord, that the plague on the people may be stopped.' Araunah said to David 'Let my lord the king take whatever pleases him and offer it up. Here are oxen for the burnt offering, and*

*here are threshing sledges and ox yokes for the wood. O
king, Araunah gives all this to the king.' Araunah also said
to him, 'May the Lord your God accept you.' But the king
replied to Araunah, 'No, I insist on paying you for it. **I will
not sacrifice to the Lord my God burnt offerings that
cost me nothing.'** (2 Sam. 24:18-24)*

True worship will always cost you something; it always involves a
sacrifice of some sort. It's interesting to note that from the beginning
of time, mankind has found an excuse to either limit, or reject,
the worship that is due God. When we choose to sin, we choose
not to give God the worship due His great name. Adam's excuse
was that someone else caused him to be disobedient. What was
Cain's excuse for not worshipping God in an acceptable way? Cain
acted like he knew better, but was going to do it his way regardless.
"Then the Lord said to Cain, 'Why are you angry? Why is your face
downcast? If you do what is right, will you not be accepted? But if
you do not do what is right, sin is crouching at your door; it desires
to have you, but you must master it.'" (Gen. 4:6-7) *Some of us have
a downcast face concerning the cost of worship in our lives.* Intimacy
requires time, humility, vulnerability, purity, and abandonment of
self. That sounds pretty expensive to me. Are you willing to pay such
a high price? It's too great of a price for many. The time factor alone
is enough for some to say "forget it".

*Intimacy requires that you wait on the Lord. As I think back to
what helped me discover and grow in intimacy, one thing sticks out in
my mind: you can't be in a hurry.* Do you remember when you were
dating? You were content to just spend hours together with that
special someone. It never occurred to you back then that you were
spending too much time together. On the contrary, you wanted
more time together. It probably seemed like you just couldn't get
enough time with each other. You invested days, months, even years
of your life. But it was worth it! Time flew by; yet it was as if time
was standing still. The world was passing you by—and you could

care less! Such is the approach you must take toward spending time with God.

REASON #3—WE ARE NOT DESPERATE

Imagine you just had a physical at the doctor's office. He steps out of the room for a few minutes, comes back in and says,

> Let me be honest with you. You are in fairly good health. Your blood pressure is normal. Your heart appears healthy. But I have one concern. You are 40 pounds overweight. I'm concerned about the effect this could potentially have on your heart. I want you to consider a change in diet, with increased exercise added to your daily routine.

So you go home and think about what the doctor said. You start to rationalize to yourself. "Well, the doctor did say I am in fairly good health. Everyone could probably stand to lose a few pounds, right? It's not like he said I'm 100 pounds overweight. As long as my heart is ok, it's all good. I'll cut back on the desserts and take a few walks—that should do it."

Did you sense any concern for urgency in the above scenario? Do you think it is out of the ordinary? When everything is going well in a man or woman's life, there is no sense of urgency. So what are we to do? Should we desire that bad times come our way, so that we can have a sense of urgency toward God? No; of course not. For most, hard times only create a sense of urgency for a limited time. The urgency lasts as long as the crisis lasts. And often the urgency is only "Lord, get me out of this." We desperately want to exit the crisis quickly. Therefore the urgency never becomes a desire to change inwardly. Rather, it merely becomes a desire to change our outward circumstances.

Desperate times call for desperate measures. Have you ever heard this saying? How true it is. I'm sure you have found it to be true, just as I have on many occasions. Regrettably, we have brought this strategy called coping into our walk with Christ. All too often we refuse to get desperate for God until we experience some sort of crisis in our life. That's why we don't pray. We're not desperate; we don't see our need. We need to be convinced. So what happens? Pain and suffering enters the door of our life, and we rush to our knees to seek our God. Then all too often, when the situation is somewhat resolved, we move on. God just gets left behind until the next crisis arises. When we avoid a life that is desperate for God, we push the prospects of intimacy out the window.

Sometimes we travel a long way just to find God. And sometimes the longer the journey—the more difficult the road—the deeper we find him. For we end up at the closing stages of our journey as a desperate, broken person. We have no more "face to save", no more dignity to maintain. We couldn't sink any lower, so we simply stop trying to pretend we can actually swim.

It's at this point that the man or woman of God clings to the garment of Jesus and refuses to let go. Remember the story? (Mark 5:24-34) Everyone in the crowd was trying to get close to Jesus. But there was a woman among them that was different from the rest. She was desperate. Many were touching Jesus, but her touch was unlike the others. Her pleading had reached the ears of her Father in heaven. Her act is a model for us of the faith walk we are to be living daily. The others in the crowd were seekers as well. Yet she went further. Her hand grasped the door handle and by faith opened the door to a room of wisdom and blessing. All of this granted to her by the grace of a merciful God.

Have you done this? Are you desperate for God today? An overcoming desire is one that won't quit. This is found in a man or woman who hungers and thirsts for God. It's this "extra" desire that helps them to overcome all obstacles in their way. Have you ever "pressed into God" like the woman in the story? Or are you simply a member of the crowd following Jesus? There's nothing wrong with that. But wouldn't you rather experience His power and have a transformed life?

Being desperate for God has little to do with your current circumstances. It's in the rendering of your heart, the deliberateness of your mind, and the obedience of your soul that desperateness occurs. You begin by placing your life in a position of need before God.

This is something that is done daily in your pursuit of Him. You don't make it happen by selling the house and quitting your job. Some people steer their boat in such a way as to avoid all contact with rough water, not to mention storms. I don't blame them. Others have just lived a life free of the presence of storms (I wish that was my life). Many have had more than their share of storms. Regardless of the hand that you believe you were dealt, having and enduring the storms of life does not automatically mean you will become desperate for God. Nor does the opposite prove true. You can be a man or woman of God whose life is storm-free, and still be one who displays desperateness in your approach to God.

The storms of life do not produce an ongoing, intimate dependence on the Lord. But they certainly create urgency. Their effect is temporary however. Once the storm passes, you often go back to the way you were living before the storm came. Yes, it changes you. But the staying power of change is rooted deeper. Those who walk daily in an attitude of desperateness for God know this staying power.

REASON #4—THERE'S NO ROOM IN OUR LIVES FOR IT

I might as well just come out and say it. We are too busy! This doesn't surprise anyone. I don't wish to debate the point, as I'm sure there is almost unmitigated agreement on this issue of busyness.

Rather than argue about whether it is right or wrong to be so busy, I'd rather state the facts. Fact #1—we don't know how to rest. Fact#2—there is no room in our lives for an intimate relationship with God because we are too busy.

"For if Joshua had given them rest, God would not have spoken later about another day. There remains, then, a Sabbath-rest for the people of God; for anyone who enters God's rest also rests from his own work, just as God did from his." (Hebrews 4:8-10) Scripture gives us a warning here. We are to hasten to enter the rest of God. "Let us, therefore, make every effort to enter that rest, so that no one will fall by following their example of disobedience." (Hebrews 4:11) There is also a warning not to miss it. "Therefore, since the promise of entering his rest still stands, let us be careful that none of you be found to have fallen short of it." (Hebrews 4:1)

Rest here represents God's provision, God's promise, and God's plan. God had provided rest for his people, Israel. Instead of entering that rest, they chose the route of unbelief. Why do I mention this portion of scripture? It's because the Bible does not give us warning without due cause. The tendency in the heart of man is to follow the same path.

When it comes to rest, we don't know what it really is. Therefore we can't enter into God's provision for our lives. We first must learn what it is; then discover how to make it happen. A whole book could be written on this topic. While it's beyond the scope of this book to adequately address such a subject, we will yet throw a few darts at the target. It affects intimacy, so I must address it. I'll give you a very simple, yet practical synopsis.

The goal is intimacy with Christ. Standing in the way of intimacy is our busyness. There's no room in our lives to enter into intimacy because we don't have the time it would take for that to occur, develop, and be sustained. Our busy lives lead to an overwhelming sense of weariness. Out of this grows an awareness of our need for rest. First, our body sends us the signals. Then our mind tells us it makes sense to get some rest. Finally, our soul hears the voice of the Spirit, and we take some much needed time off.

Recently, a brother in Christ asked me, "Have you been busy lately?" I told him, "No, I haven't been busy at all." He looked at me as if I was from some other planet. I could tell that he was frazzled, worn, and weary. His response had a hint of jealousy to it. More than anything, the look on his face was one of longing—a longing to escape the frantic pace of a busy schedule, and be content with that choice.

The problem starts here. Even when we finally rest, it's only a physical one. However, it is a spiritual rest that God is offering us. (Matt. 11:28-30) *No man understands rest until he has rested in the very arms of God Himself.* We need to cease from the <u>attitude</u> of work. Until we cease from work, we cannot enter rest. Attitude here represents a stubborn willingness to do life our way, to be in control, and attempt to please God by our work. (It's very important that you understand this.) *We need to let go of the burden of weariness that we are unable to handle and were never created to bear. Be diligent to delight yourself in the Lord. This is the only acceptable sacrifice your work can bring to God.*

When God had finished His work of creation, He rested. First, He saw that it was good, He delighted in it. (Gen. 1:4-31) *Rest is not merely ceasing from our physical labor. It is the delight that is obtained when our soul has taken its rest in God's provision, God's plan, and God's control of our lives.*

It will provide more than a refreshing of one's soul when it occurs. When weariness is replaced with joy, dancing and singing follow suit. There is no rush to take your head off your Father's chest. And work, well, let's just say that it is never the same again. The burden is gone; your Father is in control now. Intimacy invites you to dance with God, and your schedule no longer makes demands on your life. *You are no longer a slave to busyness; you have become a servant to rest.* In fact the only "demand" on your life you will feel again is the call to spend time with the Lord. Your busy life, with all its frenzied demands, will seem miles away.

REASON #5—WE DON'T THINK IT'S SOMETHING WE NEED

I'm not the world's greatest salesman for Christ, but I know someone who is. He goes by the name of Holy Spirit. Some of us figure it out early in life; for others, it takes a lifetime before they finally catch on. Catch on to what? Catch on to the fact that we desperately need God to save us. For some, their life is near its end before they are willing to finally confess their sin and bow their knee to Jesus.

Every good salesman knows that in order to make the sale, you have to convince the customer that they need what you are selling. The Holy Spirit sells us on our need for Christ and His offer of salvation. But do we heed the voice of the Spirit when it comes to His invitation for intimacy? More often than not, I think our answer is no. In fact I have written this book in the hope that all of us will allow the Holy Spirit to sell us on our need for intimacy. God shouldn't have to sell us on anything, but we are so blind to the obvious. Our sinful nature, in its various forms, wars with God and blinds us to our need for more of Him. The sad truth is we often are only willing to give God the bare minimum, when He clearly demands our all. *We are not willing to go the extra mile for God, so we never travel down the road far enough to the place where intimacy resides.*

As I stated earlier, we are convinced of our need for salvation to get into heaven. However, we're just not sold on the idea that intimacy is something we have to have in our lives. It's almost like we want it spelled out for us before we will believe it. We want the Bible to command it in black and white—"Thou shall be intimate with God". The truth is we could construe many scriptures to mean that God desires and <u>requires</u> intimacy with us. For instance, "Love the Lord your God with all your heart and with all your soul and with all your strength." (Deut. 6:5) That is intimacy! And it's not a wish list from God, it is a command.

Until you become convinced that intimacy is something you have to have, you won't take any steps toward obtaining it. If you were drowning and I reached my hand into the water to save you, your response would be instantaneous. You wouldn't ponder the offer. The desperateness of your grip on my hand would be undeniable.

Since we are not convinced of our need, we don't prevail in prayer. When we don't pray, intimacy never has its chance to form in our lives, and transform our relationship with God. Prayer loses its attractiveness to us. In the flesh, we simply are not interested in prayer. Like intimacy itself, this is a hard point to sell, for there is no true gauge we can use. We can make a list of the many benefits of prayer, but the urgency and need to pray are truly subjective (or so we think). The temporal needs of man can be satisfied by less arduous means. Why strive to see the eternal when we can effortlessly fill our lives with comfort and entertainment? When one can only see his material needs, prayer has a very limited existence in the life of the believer. *Do we really have to ask why attendance is so low at our prayer meetings? We can check our own hearts and find the answer. The sad reality is that God's people get bored, just like the rest of the world.*

So what do we do? How do we convey the need? How do we get people interested in intimacy with God? Answer: We display it! First, we live it. Then we mentor and disciple others.

REASON #6—WE SIMPLY DON'T CARE!

Now some may read the statement above and contend with me. I can hear the outcry right now—"Of course we care! What on earth are you talking about?" There isn't a single person, including myself, that doesn't get personally offended when someone insinuates that we don't care. If you are a parent, you surely have been in situations where you have pointed out the lack of caring in your child, only to have them argue the point with you.

Many would say that Christians, of all the people on the face of this earth, should be the most caring, joyful, passionate, and zealous. There is every reason to be so full of life. After all, we serve the Living God; we have His eternal Word; we live in the era of grace; and we have unfathomable riches and promises as co-heirs with Jesus our Savior. Yet, in spite of all this, believers are often indistinguishable from those in the world who don't know Christ. The passion that once flowed from their lives with the outward appearance of worship, service, and witness for God, has been replaced by a spirit of apathy.

It is a sad day indeed when all sense of urgency seems to have waned. Desire has chosen another, oft-traveled path. **When the sweetness of God's presence is limited to the Sunday morning worship experience, the believer becomes too busy for a revival, and too carefree to care if one were to occur.** Is it any surprise that the passion and zeal you and I once felt toward God has ebbed away? No one seems excited about God anymore. How do we recapture this lost passion?

This urgency and passion toward God will only become a reality in our lives when we begin to set a price-tag on its value. Whether we choose to admit it or not, we place a value upon everything in life. There is a value we place on our children, health, relationships, wealth, time, occupation, pets, etc. You name it—it has a value attributed to it. The value we attach displays how much we esteem something to be worth. If the subject matter is something we don't care for, think about much, or hold in disdain, we place a value very close to zero on it. Likewise, the things that matter most to us in life are given the greatest value, with some being valued as having a worth greater than life itself. These truths are no great revelation to most of us. We live our lives on this earth as investments. We invest our passions, desires, time, and soul in those things we value as priceless.

You may have heard the phrase "been there—done that", used by someone to indicate that they have experienced what you are talking about. The phrase conveys the sense that a person is ready to move on to something new, now that they are quite familiar with the subject at hand. It also conveys an attitude that says, "Hey, I know everything about that already."

I don't think believers would take an intentional attitude such as this toward the things of God. Yet there seems to be a prevalent existence of such an attitude that has formed in the modern-day body of Christ, regardless of intentions. It's not a spirit of indifference that grips the heart of God's people today; it's a spirit of apathy. When you show the world your attitude of "been there—done that", what are you really saying? You're saying, "I want to be entertained. I want something that's new, cutting-edge, and exciting. I need my emotions stirred. Give me something that will hold my attention and keep me interested."

Whatever happened to passion? When did desire leave the church? Why do we get excited about so little? Why does everything stir our emotions but God? Just look at our conversations. We talk about the latest blockbuster movie. We talk about the weather as if it dominates our thoughts. We celebrate sports heroes to the degree that it's no surprise our kids are more fascinated with them than God.

Why is there such a spirit of apathy in the church? Because God's people are weary! We could spend hours debating the cause for this weariness, and ask ourselves whether it is justified, but I think most would at least agree to the validity of my claim. *One can't just choose to care, and expect desire to save the day. That's because a spirit of caring is not mere words; it's a series of actions that prove the point.*

REASON #7—FEAR

I feel like I could write volumes about this subject—unfortunately! Most of it would be from painful memories and personal experience. I wish it was not so. Fear is a choice that I have entered into, again and again. But it's still just a choice for us; we can say no to it. Jesus told us we have that choice. "Let not your heart be troubled, neither let it be afraid." (John 14:27b KJV) The good news is that we don't have to live in the bondage of fear anymore. God gives us this admonition in the scriptures: "For you did not receive a spirit that makes you a slave again to fear, but you received the Spirit of sonship. And by him we cry, 'Abba, Father.'" (Rom. 8:15)

I'm sitting here thinking to myself, "Alright, what does fear have to do with preventing us from entering into intimacy?" Good question if you were wondering the same thing I was. I think the answer comes on many different levels. Fear keeps us out of close relationships. It keeps us in a place we think is safe. It keeps us caught up in ourselves, our own little world. So naturally fear would keep us from opening up to God. It would look like this for the believer who lives in fear:

> I'm afraid of getting that close to anyone. I'm afraid of being out of control, saying goodbye to me. I'm afraid of the very word intimacy. I don't think I could ever get that close to God. I would feel uncomfortable. I'm so afraid of change. I want to stay where I am.

Then that is where you will stay. Don't go there my friend. Fear is a lonely place to reside.

111

CHAPTER 11

The Echoes of Childhood

Perhaps we, who have tasted of the sweetness of God's presence and have forgotten how to laugh, are most to be pitied among men. Better to be a child, and continue in the knowledge of one, than to become an adult in name only. For if maturity breeds confidence, then the lot of Christendom is in fine hands. But if we who are believed to be mature are found only to possess the knowledge of an adult, and not the heart of a child, we fall terribly short. The echoes of childhood are not heard by those assumed to be mature; they are too distant for his mind to accept. Knowledge leads only to a wall that can never quite be climbed. Yet like a fool, he keeps on trying.

John Dawson comments on the echoes of childhood:

We look at a classroom of little kids. We look at them in their beauty, their childlike innocence, and their loveliness; and we have just the song for them. 'I'll tell you what it is, kids. You are to sing this with confidence and boldness: Jesus loves me, this I know, for the Bible tells me so.' Oh, but <u>we</u> can't sing that anymore. That's a kid's song. Our songs are all about how much we love Jesus. **But we don't celebrate God's love for us anymore because we've gone through the cruelty of**

the schoolyard, the wounds of the marketplace, and
the rejection of our relationships. No longer with
confidence can we look into the face of God. And it's
an echo of childhood, the song <u>Jesus loves me</u>.

REMEMBER YOUR BEAUTY

Have you experienced what Dawson meant by "the cruelty of
the schoolyard, the wounds of the marketplace, and the rejection
of our relationships"? I can't see how anyone could live life to the
fullest and end up having escaped these experiences. *To remember
one's beauty, you must first come to terms with accepting the fact that
you have suffered loss.* **You need to hear the sound of beauty before
the echo was established.** *What does the sound of beauty sound like?
When did it first become an "echo"? To remember will require you to
acknowledge. Acknowledge what? Acknowledge that you have beauty.*

Who needs to be reminded that they are beautiful? Answer—
those who have great beauty, yet deny it. You and I—we are the
ones who need to be reminded. I marvel at the millions who do not
consider themselves beautiful. They cannot fathom it as being true,
let alone speak such a thing. Not only do they fail to acknowledge
outward beauty, but many regard themselves as having no inward
beauty.

To remember your beauty you need to admit that you once
walked in innocence; admit that you once walked in freedom. Admit
that you once danced like a person free from all cares. Let that sink
in; reminisce a bit. This cannot be merely an intellectual nod, it has
to be personal. You have to be able to remember yourself before the
drowning of innocence that occurred in your life.

Now remember when that innocence and beauty started
to become a distant echo. Think about what caused it: painful
experiences in the schoolyard, the wounds of the marketplace, and
rejection in your relationships. *Don't meditate for hours on the hurts of*

the past. That's not going to help you at all. Just quickly admit that this beauty and innocence has been lost, and needs to be regained. Then start to develop a longing in your soul to walk once again in that freedom and innocence. Now you are closer to walking in your beauty.

ACCEPT YOUR BEAUTY

Sarah was a high school friend I was witnessing to. In a conversation we had one day, I challenged her to give her life to Jesus. She told me that she needed to find out who Sarah was first, before she could find God. Sarah wanted to find herself. She wanted to understand life, purpose, and meaning—then come to God. In a kind, yet frustrating response, I basically said "good luck". I knew well that she could spend the rest of her life searching for herself and die, never quite finding herself or God. I told her, "Come to God first, and then you can find yourself in God." We often fail to respond to what God is initiating. Sadly, we often come to God on our own terms.

Why did I tell you about Sarah? She might spend the rest of her life trying desperately to find out who she is, seeking to discover a beauty within. All of this she could find if she simply gave her life to Christ and discovered her beauty in His eyes. Listen closely. **It is not fundamentally necessary to see your beauty to receive God's salvation. Instead, you must see your nakedness; you must see yourself as a sinner. However, it is extremely fundamental to the experience of intimacy to have the ability to see yourself as beautiful in God's eyes.** Only God can give you the eyes to see yourself that way. It really comes down to accepting the truth that you are beautiful to God. Failure to do so limits your ability to develop the kind of relationship where you know God as your Lover. Do you view yourself as beautiful in God's eyes?

With tones of endearment toward their God, Christians tend to relate in terms of Savior, Lord, Father, and friend. You can experience intimacy with God in each of these four ways of relating to Him, and you should. Yet intimacy is not only relating to God in these terms, but knowing Him as your Lover as well. There comes a time and place in our life where we make a decision to move on—a decision of deeper commitment. We decide that dating God just isn't ok for us anymore. We decide to get married. We accept Jesus' invitation to be His bride.

Imagine yourself as the beauty in a dream of the Lord. Herein lies a major problem for us men. If you are a female you no doubt can conjure up a better picture than we men can. However, to be intimate with God is not to simply allow oneself to be romantic. If this were the case, a man who is far from mastering the art of romance could still stumble his way through the script. Despite stepping on the feet of our date at the dance, we would manage to get the job done, which is something all men firmly believe in.

Now picture yourself as the bride of Christ. Every hopeful bride knows the man of her dreams. They have met many times. Such hope is there that her dreams have become faith herein: she knows he exists. Her dreams have now surpassed hope. They require but one thing—the finding of her lover, the face-to-face meeting of the bride and her groom. She now dreams of what to say, how to act, and what the first encounter may hold.

The day of excitement has finally arrived. He is actually much more dashing than her dreams had allowed. How uncomfortable she feels. Sensing her own lack of security, she probes the intent of her lover's heart. "Is he pleased with me?" she asks. Her mind races to find the answer in the gaze of the bridegroom's eyes. Wrongly assuming he is disappointed, she over-compensates, striving to win his affection.

As she returns home that evening she is sure the clock will strike twelve, and she will wake up and realize it was just another dream. When the sunlight hits her face, she awakens the next morning. It was not a dream, and she is delighted to know her day has finally come. She is filled with joy and yet unsettled at the same time. "Did he think as highly of me as I did of him?" she asks. "Was he impressed by what he saw in me? I should have worn something else. I can't believe I said some of those things."

The gears in her mind are fast at work. She must discover a way to catch and hold. This one cannot get away. What a relief it will be to get down the aisle and hear him recite his vows. Then her fears will be relieved. She wishes only to hear his voice, and to see his face as he says, "Fear not my adorable bride, for your beauty has captivated me. I choose you. My vows shall I keep as a covenant of my love for you."

What am I writing about here my friends? This is not a fairy tale. This is a dream come true. And it involves you! Like the bride in this story who feels uncomfortable in the presence of her "perfect man", all of us—male and female—need to face this feeling of awkwardness if we are going to break through to intimacy. What is this feeling of awkwardness you ask? Ah, you know it well my friend. It is the feeling of awkwardness in God's presence (the presence of the perfect beauty).

It doesn't require us men taking on the role of a female. But it requires every man and woman who follows Christ to accept the role of His bride. You have already won His heart. He already calls you beautiful. That is what you said yes to at the altar. You are His beauty—accept it!

Part of accepting your beauty is to simply believe that you are beautiful. Most people don't. They won't allow themselves to do so. *To accept your beauty is to believe that you are attractive to Christ. Then you approach Him every day like you would approach someone who is incredibly attracted to you. No matter what you did or said two minutes ago, you get right back up, and approach Him like He is crazy in love with you. He is attracted to your beauty.*

It will never be accomplished by believing that beauty is something of the past. You don't regain beauty that has been lost by living in the past either. Where would you go in order to regain it? The only way to regain it is to inherit it. Innocence and beauty have been granted to you in Christ. Everyone simply receives this inheritance when they give their life to Jesus. Now you are called

God's beauty. This doesn't, however, equate to every Christian actually believing it, living it, and walking in it. You have to do your part. And doing your part will determine your ability to walk in your beauty and live a life of intimacy.

WALK IN YOUR BEAUTY

It is so fitting that we talk about the Garden of Eden as we look at how to walk in our beauty. God's design for Adam and Eve was to never possess the knowledge of evil. They were not created with perfect knowledge. It was enough for them to know God, to have an intimate relationship with Him. God was protecting their innocence in the same way we protect our children from evil influences. Because of the sin of disobedience, their beauty and innocence became lost. Thus began the quest of humanity to regain the great pearl of innocence. You can just see the struggle start to unfold as they strive to reconcile their lifestyle to the image of God that they still have, albeit in a mind that is now clouded by a tainted conscience.

Although there is no longer a Garden of Eden with an angel guarding the entrance, mankind continues to push at its gates in order to lay hold of the tree of life. With limited knowledge, and a seared conscience, their efforts are only in vain. But we have been born again. This is the precise reason we should not feel that we as believers have been shortchanged. We don't merely have the ability to regain our lost beauty and innocence. We are able to walk in it. That's why we need to listen to the echoes of childhood, because they will lead us to a place where we can learn to walk in our beauty.

If you can hear the echoes of childhood in your own ears, I invite you to take the next step with me. Are you good at finding a particular radio frequency? You turn the dial and wait about two seconds to hear the first couple words, and you know if it is a place you want to stop and listen to for awhile. It's the same with the echoes of childhood. Once you get tuned in, the songs of childhood get easier to identify. Can you hear the laughter of children? Can you feel the rush of excitement in the air? It's the expectation of something good about to happen. It's the fulfillment of the hope that has been building in your heart. Everyone is gathering to hear a story. You too will hear it if you listen as a child. Once you learn how to listen as a child, **you** will be the one telling the stories.

Here is how you walk in your beauty. It's very simple. #1 Come as a child. #2 Live as a child. Again, don't make it overly complicated. Keep it simple. *Come as a child* means to come in faith, to trust, to believe, to be excited because of your expectation of something good about to happen in your life.

Live as a child means you are secure in your beauty. You can't walk in shoes you just don't feel comfortable walking in. When you are secure in your beauty, it shows. Have you ever had a conversation with someone who just couldn't look you in the eyes the entire time? Some people are never able to look anyone in the eyes because they are ashamed of who they are. They feel so much shame that they can't see their beauty.

Not so with King David. While he was honest about the ugly sin in his life, he also knew his beauty in the eyes of his God. When he walked in beauty, others took note. People will notice you when you begin to take these steps of walking in your beauty. *It's not a beauty that flaunts; it's a beauty that gives glory to God.* David was secure in his beauty. He was unashamed to let it show. Remember when David danced before the Lord? He was walking in his beauty, that's why he was so free to dance.

> David, wearing a linen ephod, danced before the Lord with all his might, while he and the entire house of Israel brought up the ark of the Lord with shouts and the sound of trumpets. As the ark of the Lord was entering the City of David, Michal daughter of Saul watched from a window. And when she saw King David leaping

and dancing before the Lord, she despised him in her heart. (2Samuel 6:14-16)

Now this is David's wife who had a problem with him.

When David returned home to bless his household, Michal daughter of Saul came out to meet him and said, 'How the king of Israel has distinguished himself today, disrobing in the sight of the slave girls of his servants as any vulgar fellow would!' David said to Michal, '*It was before the Lord,* who chose me rather than your father or anyone from his house when he appointed me ruler over the Lord's people Israel—*I will celebrate before the Lord. I will become even more undignified than this, and I will be humiliated in my own eyes. But by these slave girls you spoke of, I will be held in honor.*' (2Samuel 6:20-22)

To the pure eyes that day, what David did was holy. *When you walk in beauty, not only are you set free, but others become inspired and are liberated as well. And most importantly, God gets all the glory.*

CHAPTER 12

When God Whispers

I find myself looking out the window, waiting for a rainbow to appear in the blue morning sky. I'm weary from days of rainfall that seem to have no end. I open the window and listen to the gentle wind. It brings no comfort to my soul. Then I hear a sound I've heard before, a melody vastly familiar to me. At once all the longings in my soul awaken. It's the voice of hope calling. "Today is a new day", God whispers. A rainbow appears out of the corner of my eye. I turn to gaze upon its beauty, and remember that whispers don't lie. God made a promise He alone can keep. When God whispers He calls my name. Help is on the way; no more living without hope. I am reminded of His love for me.

*W*hat do you envision when I write about God whispering? Do you see Him speaking something personal into your ear? Good—that's what I see too. I don't know about you, but I wouldn't whisper in just anyone's ears. I certainly wouldn't in a stranger's ears. Nor would I whisper in the ear of someone who is merely an acquaintance. Why? Because it is a gesture that you make with someone you are close to, someone you are intimate with. It is a gesture that represents trust.

So who would God whisper into the ear of? Answer: Probably someone who is intimate with Him. Definitely someone He can trust. I'm using the word trust here in a different way than you might use the word. It is not telling someone a secret in trust, hoping they will not tell anyone else. Rather, it is a matter of God knowing who He can give precious things to, because they will value and treasure them. *"The Lord confides in those who fear him; he makes his covenant known to them." (Ps. 25:14)* When you look up this word confide in a Merriam-Webster dictionary you will find "to have or show faith in; to entrust." Confide has a similarity to the word confidence, which is defined as "a state of trust or *intimacy.*" And here we see God confiding in "those who fear him." To fear God is to show Him great honor and respect. To walk in the fear of the Lord is to do this daily, not just on Sunday morning. We know from scripture what God does for those who show Him honor: He honors them. "Those who honor me I will honor, but those who despise me will be disdained." (1Sam. 2:30c) God honors that man or woman by revealing Himself, making His real presence known in their life. God confides in them; He whispers in their ears a covenant known only by those that fear Him.

Is that neat, or what? When God whispers to you—you know it. You just do. His Spirit trains you to be able to hear His voice. It is unmistakable, undeniable, and crystal clear. When you have found favor with God you will discover that the Lord often whispers into your ears. He will take you into His confidence. It's not something forced. It's not something you work up by intense effort; it will come to you as you walk in the fear of the Lord. The title of this book you are reading was whispered into my ear by God. I had already changed the title a couple times. It was nothing close to what the title is today. I was driving down the road one day, thinking about the book, and God whispered in my ear, "Call it *When Goodness Finds You*". My heart leapt with joy and excitement. I thought, "That's it! That's perfect!"

If I were to ask you what your top three favorite movies of all-time are, what would you say? Would it be something you could rattle off without thinking about it for ten minutes? There's something about movies. They have a way of grasping our attention. And not just for two hours. If we really like one we find ourselves thinking about it the next day, even telling others how much we enjoyed our experience. In fact, we have no trouble at all watching the same movie three or four times over the course of several years if we have the chance to. The movie does something for us. It captures our emotions, stirs up our passions, and helps us escape into a world of imagination. The experience is often an escape from reality, which we feel we need from time to time. It does wonders for the soul to simply relax, kick our feet up, forget about the burdens of life for awhile, and enjoy the simple pleasures of a good movie.

There is no lack of choice today when it comes to movies. We are so inundated by entertainment that we have countless options to fixate upon. We can rent a video from a vending machine as easy as getting a soda. If this doesn't flip your ignition switch you can choose from over 400 cable channels or download your entertainment fun on your own home computer, tablet, or cell phone. That's a lot of choices. Our minds spin with media overload. It is a challenge for anyone to get and keep our attention for any meaningful length of time.

Into this minefield of activity—this feeding frenzy of information sharks—strolls God. He doesn't grab the wheel and pull the emergency brakes. He doesn't sit in the backseat and wait for us to invite Him into the front. What does He do to get our attention? He whispers. Those that are wise will hear and respond. But the noise of this life is so deafening, and the allurement of this world so captivating, it silences the voice of God in our lives. There are so many other things to do. We simply change the channel until we find something we really like, something that can hold our attention and spark our passion.

So God ends up having to compete for our time and attention with all the multimedia draws that pervade our culture. But He doesn't. He won't compete with anyone or anything for our time, passion, or love. He waits patiently and whispers. Sometimes I wish it was more than a whisper. But that is what a gentle, loving Father does. Do you want to hear God whisper in your ears? Walk in the fear of the Lord: Honor Him above everything else in your life. Turn off the noise that competes for God's time. Wait on Him; quiet yourself before Him. Then begin to listen. When you have a heart that seeks after God, a heart that honors Him and His children, you will find God's favor. Then it's time to bend your ear, because someone special is about to whisper and confide in you.

CHAPTER 13

When Goodness Finds You

When the music fades and the worship ceases... when the fellowship ring is broken... when your calendar is void of activity, your friends stop calling, and no one seems to care... when all you can feel is pain, and trials have overtaken you... when your prayers have turned to pleas, with loneliness your only roommate... oh beautiful bride, where do you turn?

The soul was designed for such a day as this. You and I were created for such a God as this. With nowhere else to turn, and nothing else divine, the soul has but one choice, to seek rest in its Maker. Intimacy with God is often found through anguish of soul and loneliness, more so than it is through laughter, contentment, and fellowship. Yet it cannot grow or thrive in a continued state of anguish or loneliness. There must be an experience of God's goodness.

*I*n his bestselling classic <u>The Knowledge Of The Holy</u>, A. W. Tozer writes about the many attributes of God, including His goodness. Tozer states,

> To allow that God could be other than good is to deny the validity of all thought and end in the negation of every moral judgment. If God is not good, then there

can be no distinction between kindness and cruelty, and heaven can be hell and hell, heaven. *The goodness of God is the drive behind all the blessings He daily bestows upon us.* God created us because He felt good in His heart and He redeemed us for the same reason.[8]

Believers often speak of the day they "found Jesus". This statement begs the question "Where was He hiding?" One never really finds grace—grace finds us. Mercy finds us; we receive the free gift. Can God's goodness actually find you? What is goodness? How does it find you? Not only can it find you, it can become a part of you. You can live your life surrounded by God's goodness. What does that look like? Don't make it too complicated. It's not a secret formula tucked away in a vault, behind locked doors.

It is easy to believe that all Christians upon being asked the question, "Is God good?" would answer yes. But how many actually believe it in the context of their reality? How many believers, God's own children, actually believe God has dealt them a bad hand? In other words—God is good—but not to us—at least not right now—but yeah, He's good. Most would never admit to it, of course, but yet they believe some form of this in their hearts. Usually it comes out of their mouths this way: "Yes, of course God is good...but..." What follows this statement is often a long explanation of troubles that they, as well as others they have known, have experienced.

Recently I had such a conversation with an acquaintance I have known for many years. This man is a very strong believer, as well as a Bible teacher. I asked him, "Do you believe that God is good?" He looked at me and hesitated. That was enough to shock me right there. He said, "Well, can you define good?" I had hope that he was kidding, but soon realized from the look on his face that he was not. What ensued was a lengthy conversation about God's goodness. But behind his question were statements which he vigorously defended,

---

8   A. W. Tozer, *The Knowledge Of The Holy* (San Francisco: Harper & Row, 1961), 135.

foremost being this belief that God for some unbeknownst reason sends bad things our way.

Many believe their circumstances in life right now are not fair. They don't know why, but believe that God has allowed them to be destroyed, their lives ruined, in order to teach them something. That's a lie! Your heavenly Father is not the destroyer. Neither does He team up with the devil to mess up your life. "The thief comes only to steal and kill and destroy; **I have come that they may have life, and have it to the full.**" (John 10:10)

Let me be plain with you. It is way beyond the scope of this book as well as the desire of this author to address (or try to address) the doctrinal issues raised by the question "Why do bad things happen to good people?" I don't even like the question. I prefer to focus on God's goodness, no matter how my circumstances in life try to distract me. Besides, I don't know the answer to the question, and neither do you. Some people live like they are expecting to experience bad things in their life. I'm not. I get up every morning expecting to experience something good in my life—and you should too. That's because God's thoughts toward you are good—always good. And His plan for your life is a good one—even if you don't know what that is—God does. (Jer. 29:11)

Are you looking for God's goodness in your life? Do you want goodness to find you? *Find favor with God by walking in ways that please Him, and goodness will come knocking at your door.* I put all my hope in God being good to me. I'm going to brag about how good He really is until I'm blue in the face.

We are talking about the need to experience God's goodness to facilitate walking in intimacy with Him. Three examples of intimacy from the scriptures come to my mind, where God showed favor to someone because of their relationship with Him (Moses, Job, and David). The first was Moses. Scripture tells us, "The Lord would speak to Moses face to face, as a man speaks with his friend." (Exodus 33:11) When you are intimate with God, it gives you great confidence before Him. You can approach Him with confidence, knowing that you have His favor. "If you are pleased with me, teach me your ways so I may know you and continue to find favor with you", Moses said. (Ex. 33:13) "And the Lord said to Moses, 'I will do the very thing you have asked, because I am pleased with you and I know you by name.'" (Ex. 33:17) What resulted was the Lord revealing His glory to Moses and allowing all of His goodness to pass before him. What an incredible blessing!

When God is pleased with you, He sends goodness your way.

> Then Moses said, 'Now show me your glory.' And the Lord said, 'I will cause all my goodness to pass in front of you, and I will proclaim my name, the Lord, in your presence. I will have mercy on whom I will have mercy, and I will have compassion on whom I will have compassion.' (Ex. 33:18-19)

Moses had asked the Lord to show him the glory of God. God responded by showing Moses His goodness. *What was God saying? He was saying that His glory is His goodness! And He reveals this goodness to those who please Him, and to those He knows by name. This is how God treats those who are intimate with Him.*

Job believed in God's goodness also. He certainly experienced it. Even Satan commented on the abundance of goodness that was poured out on Job. "Does Job fear God for nothing?" Satan replied. "Have you not put a hedge around him and his household and everything he has? You have blessed the work of his hands, so that his flocks and herds are spread throughout the land." (Job 1:9-10)

Then something happened to Job. Not just the obvious external circumstances, but inwardly. Job began to question God's goodness, justice, and judgment. Job said,

> Though I cry, 'I've been wronged!' I get no response; though I call for help, there is no justice. He has blocked my way so I cannot pass; he has shrouded my paths in darkness. He has stripped me of my honor and removed

the crown from my head. He tears me down on every side till I am gone; **he uproots my hope like a tree.** (Job 19:7- 10)

When you or I start talking or thinking like this, we cut ourselves off from God's goodness. There is no way we can experience God's goodness in this state. Job complained that God had taken away his hope. Since hope is exactly what a person needs, Job made a huge mistake by accusing God of removing that from him. *Don't limit the goodness of God in your life by judging God as unfaithful to you.* Believe instead like the psalmist David, "I am still confident of this: I will see the goodness of the Lord in the land of the living." (Psalm 27:13) Where is the land of the living? That's where you live! We are not talking about some day in the distant future when you get to heaven. That's here! That's now! Of course you will experience God's great goodness in heaven. But David believed to experience it right here—right now. We must do the same.

<u>When Goodness Finds You</u> is not about enabling you to have an experience that will change your life for a moment. Christianity is not meant to be an experience. It is all about a relationship. Intimacy brings a unique element into that relationship. That element is God's goodness. *Intimacy gives us the confidence to look God in the eyes and know in our heart that He is thinking something good about us.*

I find myself choosing to sing a familiar song over and over again. It's a song about the goodness of God. I first learned the song over 25 years ago in a college Christian fellowship group. It's a song I sang over my children when they were little, as I stood by their crib in the early hours of the morning, trying to settle them down and get them to sleep. It reminds me that God has been good to me before, and He will again. I simply refuse to give up until I see and experience the same goodness that David saw and experienced. He said, "Surely goodness and love will follow me all the days of my life, and I will dwell in the house of the Lord forever." (Psalm 23:6) David believed that goodness would follow right after him;

he expected good things to happen in his life on a regular basis. Do you?

This has become my own saying that I believe God has given me. You can say it with me and make it yours as well. It goes like this: "I got *just* enough faith—to believe that God is—*just* that good—that He would do something—*just* that wonderful—for me!"

So how does goodness find us? It follows after those who please God. He pours it out on those who take refuge in Him. "How great is your goodness, which you have stored up for those who fear you, which you bestow in the sight of men on those who take refuge in you." (Psalm 31:19) Just how great is God? He stores up goodness for us! Stores it up? That's mind-boggling. A lot of parents, of course, store up wealth for their kids. God is no different—only much, much better.

When you experience God's goodness, it becomes something more to you than a daily journal entry, or fond memory. It forms the framework for intimacy. I remember one such experience several years ago. I had been seeking God earnestly about a financial need that I had. I was crying out to Him day and night. One afternoon, after pouring out my heart before the Lord, I felt a sense of peace in my heart. I believed everything was going to be okay, and that the money I needed was on its way. I knew it was just a matter of time. A week later, I came home from work and was looking at the mail when a letter caught my eye. I started thinking, "why did I get something from this person?" Right then the presence of God came upon me real strong. I knew in my spirit what was in the letter before I opened it. It was the answer to my prayers. My provision was inside. Inside the letter, which came through an unexpected avenue, was a check for one thousand dollars! I found myself caught between whether I should cry, shout, or praise the Lord. So I did every one of them. *When God comes through for you and reveals His goodness, it means more to you than precious diamonds or fine gold. The experience of God's goodness is simply priceless. When goodness finds you, you receive a much needed breakthrough. You experience the God who is more than just enough—He's simply too much!*

CHAPTER 14

The Joy of Breakthrough

There have come and gone multitudes of dreamers upon this earth, some of great stature, some of small. Those that dream have been found among nobility and common folk, rich and poor, the faithful and the wicked, the hopeful and the hopeless. I wish to be counted among them. Born a dreamer and always a dreamer, I have found myself caught up in something far greater. You and I, whether we like it or not, are a part of something far bigger than we could ever imagine. We are front and center in our Father's dreams. In the middle of a mystery, part of an ever unfolding plot, you and I have been plucked from our humdrum existence, given a new name, and dropped into the midst of a growing storybook.

Heroes and heroines, we play the part of the rescuer and the rescued, the fearful and the fearless, and oddly enough, the blessed <u>and</u> the afflicted. Not knowing our true name or the fullness of our identity, we stumble through the plot. Some grasp desperately at the present, while others cling to the past. Yet all are aware of the certainty of the ending. Our lines are read with faith, not omniscience, therefore our control lies only in the clarity of our voice, the dignity of our character, and the passion of our role playing. Never do we see the complete unveiling of our character or the fate of his existence.

This, of course, is reserved for the Teller of Stories, the Maker of Dreams. Our own dreams are only a reality when their actions become realized as part of a microcosm. Then they become truth: a dream fulfilled, an adventure experienced, a wish granted. They become swallowed up in the macrocosm of what is better known as <u>God's will</u>. Dreams that never end only become greater realities.

No man dreams outside of God. No plans are wrought without His understanding. Though many, yea, the saints of God, stray from the main story, He alone reserves the right to edit. Indeed, men move freely throughout the story, yet unaware of the hidden hand that moves them along. Their justice is neither limited by the foolish fatalist nor enhanced by the playful schemer. "In his heart a man plans his course, but the Lord determines his steps." (Prov. 16:9)

The hands that move, the Judge who judges, and the Lawgiver who shows mercy are none other than the Creator Himself. In light of Him, the playwright, the puppeteer, and the chess-master forfeit control. Only the Just Creator could bless the hero <u>and</u> the villain. Neither leaves His sight. "The eyes of the Lord are everywhere, keeping watch on the wicked and the good." (Prov. 15:3)

*I*t's much easier to go to church than it is to fall on our knees and seek God. Revival starts in a man's heart. So many come to church not expecting anything to be different. Desire is at hand, but there is no expectation of a breakthrough. That's because nothing is different in their lives. It's the same old routine that it was last week and last month. But when you have a building full of people who are experiencing revival in their hearts—then you have church.

It is a powerful thing when you have people who actually come to church expecting God to move—to be what He said He would be—to do what He said He would do—on behalf of His people. Then you have children who are hungry and thirsty for their Father's presence, showing up in eagerness, believing God is going to do something good. That's when the anointing falls; God reveals Himself; He touches and changes lives. People leave full of God, and can't wait to return to God's house next week.

We tend to think that someday we will just wake up on the other side of happiness, and everything will be just perfect in our lives; we will be at the place we want to be; we will really care about the things that matter the most. *But life is not a series of passionate pleas, emotional responses, and altar calls. The person who lives their life this way wakes up one day and realizes that life has passed them by. The opportunity has come and gone. This person stares into the mirror of their life and wonders where the time has gone. With urgency they exclaim, "I'm ready to care now. I'm ready to get serious about God." But like a child trying to avert punishment for disobedience, the response is shallow and short-lived.* What this person I describe desperately needs is a breakthrough.

There's something about experiencing God that is transformational. It doesn't validate God's reality, or ability, or the credibility of His Word. It changes us. In order for this experience of God to become something on-going and foundational, you must develop intimacy. You know Him as your Savior and Lord, but you must get to know Him as your breakthrough. He must become your salvation. He already is your Savior based on Christ's finished work at the cross. You have made it personal by receiving this free gift. But in your experience of Him, He must become salvation for you in your everyday reality.

God delivered His people Israel from the bondage of Egypt. He performed a miracle, parted the Red Sea, and the Israelites walked through the sea on dry land.

> Then Moses and the Israelites sang this song to the Lord:
> 'I will sing to the Lord, for he is highly exalted. The horse

and its rider he has hurled into the sea. The Lord is my strength and my song; *he has become my salvation.* He is my God, and I will praise him, my father's God, and I will exalt him. The Lord is a warrior; the Lord is his name.' (Ex. 15:1-3)

Israel knew the Lord as their strength and song, but now He was known by a new name among them. It wasn't until then that they knew God's salvation. The Israelites were saying,

For many years we would sing songs to you; in fact, you are our song—the song of our hearts. And you are the one we trust in—you are our strength! But now we know you in a new way. *You have become our salvation. We now know you as the God of breakthrough.*

Some of you have been looking for a breakthrough in your life for years. You are well acquainted with heartache, and desire above all else to finally experience God's salvation in the area of your greatest need. The Lord wants you to know Him as the God of breakthrough. So He repeats this message in the book of Isaiah, giving you hope that you too can experience Him in this way. God gives us a glimpse of what that day will look like.

In that day you will say: 'I will praise you, O Lord. Although you were angry with me, your anger has turned away and you have comforted me. Surely God is my salvation; I will trust and not be afraid. *The Lord, the Lord, is my strength and my song; he has become my salvation.'* With joy you will draw water from the wells of salvation. (Isaiah 12:1-3)

Experiencing the joy of breakthrough is a necessity to intimacy with God. One of the realities that I have come to learn about breakthroughs is that it's not so much me breaking through, as it is God breaking through. Thank God for that. Sometimes the wall that seems to keep us from any victory or breakthrough is just too big to climb. If you feel like you are at the end of your rope—hold on. Meditate on the words of Psalm 118.

> In my anguish I cried to the Lord, and he answered by setting me free. *I was pushed back and about to fall, but the Lord helped me. **The Lord is my strength and my song; he has become my salvation.** Shouts of joy and victory resound in the tents of the righteous: 'The Lord's right hand has done mighty things! The Lord's right hand is lifted high; the Lord's right hand has done mighty things!' I will not die but live, and will proclaim what the Lord has done.* (Psalm 118:5; 13-17)

IS GOD SOMETHING ELSE, OR WHAT?

That God—He is something else, isn't He? Boy, He's quite the God, huh? I'm not trying to be disrespectful here. I'm sure you have heard this phrase before, just not with God in it. I remember hearing it often with my name in it; usually with the added "you are quite the character". The phrase is often used when men shake their head in astonishment, and laugh at the uniqueness of someone or something they have just observed. *When you experience the joy of breakthrough, you fall in love with the God who is just something else.*

God is really something else. Nothing like we have ever known. We have nothing and no one to relate Him to. That's why the Father sent Jesus—so we could know this God who is like no other. Our soul longs for another day, just one more day. The soul was designed for something greater—not just something different—something greater—something else.

It is so much fun when God reveals Himself in simple, little ways. It's often in a way that wouldn't mean much to someone else, but to you it meant the world. You treasure it. It's the way of intimacy. When it happens in my life, I just shake my head and say, "God, you are something else."

I had just that kind of experience a year ago. During the last several years, I have spent a lot of time reading, studying, and meditating on the book of Psalms. On this particular day, I remember having what I would call a wonderful time in prayer. I was thinking about God's goodness, and I was soaking it in as well. I was talking to God about my desire to experience a greater measure of His goodness.

As I finished praying I reached for my Bible. My plan was to turn to the book of Psalms, where I have done a lot of highlighting over the years. I have plenty of favorites, and often read those passages again to encourage myself. So I'm reaching for my Bible, and God whispers to me: "sixty-eight". It wasn't an audible voice, but the thought came into my mind. This doesn't happen often to me, but it was very real. I stopped and thought, "sixty-eight?" I paused for a minute. "Am I missing something here? I don't have any favorite verses in psalm sixty-eight. I don't want to turn there; maybe that's not right." So I asked the Lord, "God, you know what my favorite verses are. Do you really want me to read psalm 68? All of your Word is wonderful, but I would rather read something else."

Have you ever just opened the Bible and started reading wherever your eyes hit the page? Often you are very excited before you start reading, and taking this approach can mean reading something that just doesn't excite you at all. In fact Psalm 68 says, "Surely God will crush the heads of his enemies, the hairy crowns of those who go on in their sins...that you may plunge your feet in the blood of your foes, while the tongues of your dogs have their share." (Psalm 68:21; 23) These are probably not the verses that would have a person doing cartwheels and shouting! In view of the fact that I had just been praying and thinking about God's goodness, this would not have been the icing on the cake. Well, I was planning on reading Psalm 68, but I never got there. I opened the Bible, and set my eyes on the first verse I saw. I had no idea what or where I was opening it to. The pages parted at Psalm 119—you guessed it—verse 68. It says, "You are good, and what you do is good." That was all I needed to read for the day. I closed the Bible back up and said, "God, are you kidding me? That's just like you to do something like that. Lord, you are so good! You are the God who is really something else!"

King David knew the God of something else. In the midst of punishing David, God reveals His heart in a most generous way. You know the story. David sins with Bathsheba; God sends the prophet Nathan to rebuke David. God's way of dealing with David, even in the midst of his punishment, was wonderful. God revealed Himself as loving, vulnerable, and completely approachable. Remember that God and David were in covenant together. They had an intimate relationship. That's why it hurt God so much. That's why God said to David, "Now, therefore, the sword will never depart from your house, because *you despised me* and took the wife of Uriah the Hittite to be your own." (2Sam. 12:10) David didn't just reject God's Word, like King Saul did when he disobeyed the Lord. This went far beyond that. David actually despised God Himself, treating their covenant like it was meaningless.

Even when He is deeply hurt, God is still love. And love does what love is—it reaches out with open arms. Most of us loving, godly parents would stick our finger in the face of our kids and say, "How dare you? Is this how you treat us? You're not even thankful for all that we have done for you. After everything we have given you, you go out and do something like this." Not so with God. He reminds David of what He gave him. But then God adds this: *"And if all this had been too little, I would have given you even more."* (2Sam. 12:8c)

What kind of God does that? A good God! He is the God of something else—that's who He is—that's who He has always been. God was saying to David,

> I made you king. I gave you Saul's palace and servants. I gave you a bunch of beautiful women to be your wives. I gave you an entire nation, and they bow their knee

before you. But even if this was not enough in your eyes David, you could have asked me, and I would have given you even more.

He is the God of too much! He is the God who fills your cup and just keeps pouring until it overflows! David was very familiar with *When Goodness Finds You*.

BUCKET LIST

Have you heard of the phrase "bucket list"? Perhaps you saw the movie by the same title, as I did. It seems to be a popular saying these days. A bucket list is a list of things you wish to do or accomplish before you die (or kick the bucket, as they say).

Perhaps you have one yourself. Here's something for you to meditate upon: Could God possibly have His own bucket list? What would be on God's bucket list concerning you? You might think that is silly or far-fetched. I don't. Look at Hebrews 6:13. "When God made his promise to Abraham, since there was no one greater for him to swear by, he swore by himself." In other words, instead of "so help me, God", God says "so help me—me!" Hey, He's God—He can do that sort of thing. If He can do that, why can't God have His own bucket list?

Imagine God Himself having a list of dreams and desires for His own children. Perhaps your name is on God's bucket list with an asterisk next to it. Next to your name are written the things God has specifically called you to do in obedience to Him. He is expecting you to fulfill His plan for your life, and God will help you to achieve this. But then there is a comment, a small notation written by the hand of your Father God. It says, "I wish they would go beyond what I have asked of them and do this (we see several items written on God's wish list)...and I wish they would do it just because they love me!"

Did you know that God keeps a diary? We all know what a diary is. It contains fond memories of everyday life, daily memoirs meant to be savored and reminisced with great joy. What do you think God records? You guessed it—stories about His kids. I will give you three Bible references. The first is <u>The Book of Life</u>. (Rev. 20:15) Everyone who is special to God (and saved), has their name written in it. The second is found in the book of Psalms. "You saw me before I was born. The days allotted to me had all been recorded in your book, before any of them ever began." (Psalm 139:16 GNT) It looks like God has been writing about us long before we ever took our first breath.

The third reference is a personal favorite of mine. "Then those who honored the Lord spoke with each other, and the Lord listened and heard them. The names of those who honored the Lord and respected him were written in his presence in a book to be remembered." (Malachi 3:16 NCV) We see here how God treasures those who honor Him in a special way. This is true intimacy with God.

> They will be my people, says the Lord of Heaven's Armies. On the day when I act in judgment, they will be my own special treasure. I will spare them as a father spares an obedient child. Then you will again see the difference between the righteous and the wicked, between those who serve God and those who do not. (Mal. 3:17-18 NLT)

God takes the opportunity to record these special moments in His own book. He says to His angels,

> *Hey, look at what my kids just did! Aren't they special? Then clapping His hands, God says, 'Quick, get my book! Write this down right now in my presence. I want this recorded for all of eternity, this moment in time. I want to savor the fragrance of the love my sons and daughters have for me.'*

He gathers the angels together to show them His book full of pictures, and details of the things His children have done for Him. With God's ability to remember, He can recall special moments like they are just happening right now before His very eyes.

Oh, to be used of God to complete His bucket list! What a dream that would be. We are talking about breakthroughs, aren't we? To break through every wall; to go beyond that which was expected of us; to fulfill our Father's plans, dreams, and desires; to do all of this just because we love Him. Talk about the ultimate way to finish your life! It sounds like the ultimate way to finish this book. God always seems to save the best for last. *Let Goodness Find You, and you may find yourself on God's bucket list—fulfilling His dreams—making God's wish come true!*

ABOUT THE AUTHOR

A teacher at heart, Scott Boucher loves to inspire others to experience the freedom that intimacy with God provides. He has been involved in numerous aspects of Church ministry for over 30 years. He served as Administrator of Mount Carmel Bible Institute from 2004-2006. More than anything, Scott is a man who simply adores  God, and enjoys spending time with Him. Scott and his wife, Mary, live in Menasha, Wisconsin, with their two children, Josiah and Victoria, and one adorable cat, Macy.

If your church or organization would like to host a seminar taught by Scott on Intimacy with God, you may contact him at (920) 637-1002. For more detailed information on seminar topics, check out *When Goodness Finds You* on facebook. Mailing address for correspondence:

WHEN GOODNESS FINDS YOU
1196 Loretta Ave
Menasha, WI 54952

All other inquiries: email Scott at Juniorsdad1@sbcglobal.net